The Wayward Genius of Henry Mayhew

The Wayward Genius of Henry Mayhew

Pioneering Reportage from Victorian London

Edited by Karl Sabbagh

Published by Hesperus Press Limited
28 Mortimer Street, London W1W 7RD
www.hesperuspress.com

London Labour and the London Poor first published in 1851
This edition first published by Hesperus Press Limited, 2012
Introduction © Karl Sabbagh, 2012

Designed and typeset by Fraser Muggeridge studio
Printed in Jordan by Jordan National Press

ISBN: 978-1-84391-378-8

Contents

Introduction

Henry Mayhew was born 200 years ago, in November 1812, the same year as his friend Charles Dickens. In personality, temperament and physical type he was very different from Dickens, although in his writings he was as prolific. He also covered similar territory to Dickens, literally as well as figuratively. Both men delighted in roaming the streets of London, and acquired a knowledge of the city and its people that infused their work.

But one difference between the two men is revealed in their funerals. Even though both were attended by a handful of mourners, in Dickens' case this was by choice; with Mayhew it was because he was largely forgotten. Once Dickens' formal funeral was over in Westminster Abbey, the grave was left open for the thousands of people who had clamoured to attend. Mayhew was buried in Kensal Green cemetery, the ceremony attended only by his son-in-law, and no one clamoured to see his grave.

And yet, as I hope to show in this small selection from Mayhew's output, his writing had much in common with Dickens'. It has even been suggested that, since Dickens knew Mayhew and read what he wrote, some of Dickens' characters are based on, or derived from, the interviews Mayhew carried out with 500 or so poor working people in the streets of London.

Mayhew's classic study of London working life, *London Labour and the London Poor,* consists of almost two million closely printed words, in the only full edition that has ever been published. Mayhew intended his work – the result of a decade roaming the streets of London talking to workers, beggars and tradesmen – to be a definitive study of a group of people who in the first half of the nineteenth century made up a majority of the population of London but were deemed unimportant by the opinion formers of the time.

Today we would call his study 'sociology' although at the time the word hadn't been invented. We would also, today, say that his study had failed, at least that it had failed to achieve Mayhew's own objectives. A wayward genius, co-founder and first editor of *Punch*, argumentative and financially uncontrollable, Mayhew thought that the researches he carried out into such topics as the weight of horse and cow manure deposited on the streets of London in a year would be a major contribution to the study of the great metropolis. In fact, his most significant contribution has been to bring to life the people of London through over 500 transcribed interviews, some of a few hundred words, others of several thousand.

There is some discussion among academics about how much Mayhew shaped the words he 'recorded'. It certainly seems from what we know about his working methods that he used stenographers or wrote down himself a faithful account of what he heard. But one writer says:

> Mayhew's artistry manifests itself above all in the shaping of his characters' monologues. As a dramatizer of character through speech, Mayhew is as superior to the tape recorder as Hamlet is to the ordinary run of Danish princes. He does not distort, but he edits, shapes, and intensifies until we are stunned by the slang beauty and inventiveness of the spoken voices he recreates. His years of editorial experience, his nose for animal effluvia, his ear for quirks of speech, his novelist's eye for significant detail ... all found the richest possible field for exercise in the inventively vociferous streets of London. The bardic speech of much Victorian verse is further from true poetry than the idiom of Mayhew's costermongers and peep-showmen.

The analogy with poetry suggests that Mayhew should be credited with evolving a new art form, a kind of dramatic monologue in prose.[1]

Another commentator has suggested that '[T]he lives written up in the text were selected and reworked for melodramatic ends. Bold characters, pathos and "human interest" were now chosen.'[2]

There are two reasons why I think Mayhew did not consciously shape his interview material for some specific effect, 'reworking for melodramatic ends'. The first is that I am not sure he was capable of that degree of control over the material he published. He was pretty disorganised in his life, and also in his writing, with *London Labour and the London Poor* going off in all directions and lacking the focused structure he intended to give it as set out in the first few pages of the work. And he seemed to gather so much material, which must have covered thousands of pages of notebooks, that it is unlikely that he sat down with drafts of his books and articles and read them all over again to give them the kind of 'editing, shaping and intensifying' that Rosenberg, for example, suggests. He even allowed one of his books, *The Great World of London*, to finish in mid-sentence. (A note by the publisher in a second edition suggests that this was 'in consequence of Mr Mayhew's absence from England'.)[3]

The second reason I trust the veracity of the interviews is that, as a documentary director who has filmed many interviews with 'real' people, I recognise in Mayhew's material the way people think and speak on their feet. These people speak like individuals who have just been accosted by a portly stranger and who are kind enough to respond to his questions, without much forethought, and with the kind of disjointed thinking that leads them suddenly to say 'And another thing' and introduce a new topic which is not always relevant to the questions they were asked. When I produced a dramatisation of eight Mayhew interviews for BBC television in 1994, the outpouring of very favourable viewer reactions was derived almost entirely from a response to the realism of the dialogue, as if these Victorian street people had been brought to life in front of their eyes.

Mayhew's approach was disorganised, and as a result, richly informative. He plunged into his interviews with little preparation, deliberately, I feel, because he wanted to get a vivid and accurate account of what people wanted to tell him rather than coach them to supply what they thought he wanted. As a result, the interviews leap off the page with an immediacy that Mayhew's own more analytical text lacks.

Some of the many interesting interviews Mayhew conducted have been published elsewhere, most recently by Hesperus Press[4] but also in various forms and selections by other publishers. For this book, I have concentrated less on the interviews and more on the surrounding material, in which he describes the streets, houses, clothes and communities of London, selecting passages that show the variety of styles Mayhew used when writing his own words rather than when he quoted others.

The original idea of using these interviews merely to gather data – about wages, trading practices, turnover, and so on – evaporated as people spoke to Mayhew about religion, marriage, childhood, illness and disability, class structures, entertainment, clothing, poverty, sex, crime and fate. He couldn't resist putting it all down and, as a result, what might have been a small contribution to the study of Victorian commerce became a unique record of the lives and preoccupations of ordinary people in their own words.

What Mayhew also couldn't resist, or perhaps couldn't help, was including vivid and novelistic – one might today say cinematic – descriptions of the scenes and people he sought out or came across fortuitously during his researches. It is these passages which complement the interviews and put them in context, showing that he was a great writer as well as a great reporter. In fact he had written novels, some with his brother Augustus, as well as a range of other books, both fiction and non-fiction, but none has had the acclaim or the durability of *London Labour and the London Poor*. His writing was as disorganised as his life, which included failed or half-completed enterprises, a bankruptcy, a failed marriage, fallings out with his father, and broken friendships even though, in the words of one writer, 'he was a genius, a fascinating companion, and a man of inexhaustible resource and humour'.

My intentions for the reader are to induce in him or her the same reaction that W.M. Thackeray had on reading Mayhew's writings when first published in the *Morning Chronicle*. This is what he wrote:

A clever and earnest-minded writer gets a commission from the *Morning Chronicle* newspaper, and reports upon the state of our poor in London: he goes among labouring people and poor of all kinds – and brings back what? A picture of human life so wonderful, so awful, so piteous and pathetic, so exciting and terrible, that readers of romances own they never read anything like to it; and that the griefs, struggles, strange adventures here depicted exceed anything that any of us could imagine.[5]

The Wayward Genius of Henry Mayhew

Chapter One: Journey into Jacob's Island

One of Mayhew's earliest accounts of a visit to a deprived area of London appeared in the Morning Chronicle *on Monday 24 September 1849, with the title 'Visit to the Cholera Districts of Bermondsey'. He had been sent by the newspaper to write about a site of a recent cholera outbreak, on the south side of the Thames at Bermondsey. This was the earliest published piece of Mayhew's writing which had the style that was to dominate his coverage of London life. As Anne Humpherys has described it: 'He combined his eye for physical detail and his sensitivity to language and wrote in a coolly factual style which is almost like the language of the physical sciences in its preciseness, accuracy, and lack of emotional bias. Yet the description is profoundly moving.'[6]*

There is an Eastern fable which tells us that a certain city was infested by poisonous serpents that killed all they fastened upon; and the citizens, thinking them sent from Heaven as a scourge for their sins, kept praying that the visitation might be removed from them, until scarcely a house remained unsmitten. At length, however, concludes the parable, the eyes of the people were opened; for, after all their prayers and fastings, they found that the eggs of the poisonous serpents were hatched in the muck-heaps that surrounded their own dwellings.

The history of the late epidemic, which now seems to have almost spent its fatal fury upon us, has taught us that the masses of filth and corruption round the metropolis are, as it were, the nauseous nests of plague and pestilence. Indeed, so well known are the localities of fever and disease, that London would almost admit of being mapped out pathologically, and divided into its morbid districts and deadly cantons. We might lay our fingers on the Ordnance map, and say here is the typhoid parish, and there the ward of cholera; for as truly as the West-end rejoices in the title of Belgravia, might the southern shores of the Thames be christened Pestilentia. As season follows season, so does disease follow disease in the quarters that may be more literally than metaphorically styled the plague-spots of London. If the seasons are favourable, and typhus does not bring death to almost every door, then influenza and scarlatina fill the work-houses with the families of the sick. So certain and regular are the diseases in their returns, that each epidemic, as it comes back summer after summer, breaks out in the self-same streets as it appeared on its former visit, with but this slight difference, that if at its last visitation it began at the top of the street, and killed its way down, this time it begins at the bottom, and kills its way as surely up the lines of houses.

Out of the 12,800 deaths which, within the last three months, have arisen from cholera, 6,500 have occurred on the southern shores of the Thames; and to this awful number no localities have contributed so largely as Lambeth, Southwark and Bermondsey, each, at the height of the disease, adding its hundred victims a week to the fearful catalogue of mortality. Any one who has ventured a visit to the last-named of these places in particular, will not wonder at the ravages of the pestilence in this malarious quarter, for it is bounded on the north and east by filth and fever, and on the south and west by want, squalor, rags and pestilence. Here stands, as it were, the very capital of cholera, the Jessore of London – JACOB'S ISLAND, a patch of ground insulated by the common sewer. Spared by the fire of London, the houses and comforts of the people in this loathsome place have scarcely known any improvement since that time. The place is a century behind even the low and squalid districts that surround it.

In the days of Henry II, the foul stagnant ditch that now makes an island of this pestilential spot, was a running stream, supplied with the waters which poured down from the hills about Sydenham and Nunhead, and was used for the working of the mills that then stood on its banks. These had been granted by charter to the monks of St Mary and St John, to grind their flour, and were dependencies upon the Priory of Bermondsey. Tradition tells us that what is now a straw yard skirting the river, was once the City Ranelagh, called 'Cupid's Gardens', and that the trees, which are now black with mud, were the bowers under which the citizens loved, on the sultry summer evenings, to sit beside the stream drinking their sack and ale. But now the running brook is changed into a tidal sewer, in whose putrid filth staves are laid to season; and where the ancient summer-houses stood, nothing but hovels, sties, and muck-heaps are now to be seen.

Not far from the Tunnel there is a creek opening into the Thames. The entrance to this is screened by the tiers of colliers which lie before it. This creek bears the name of the Dock Head. Sometimes it is called St Saviour's, or, in jocular allusion to the odour for which it is celebrated, Savory Dock. The walls of the warehouses on each side of this muddy stream are green and slimy, and barges lie beside them, above which sacks of corn are continually dangling from the cranes aloft. This creek was once supplied by the streams from the Surrey hills, but now nothing but the drains and refuse of the houses that have grown up round about it thickens and swells its waters.

On entering the precincts of the pest island, the air has literally the smell of a graveyard, and a feeling of nausea and heaviness comes over any one unaccustomed to imbibe the musty atmosphere. It is not only the nose, but the stomach, that tells how heavily the air is loaded with sulphuretted hydrogen; and as soon as you cross one of the crazy and rotting bridges over the reeking ditch, you know, as surely as if you had chemically tested it, by the black colour of what was once the white-lead paint upon the door-posts and window-sills, that the air is thickly charged with this deadly gas. The heavy bubbles which now and then rise up in the water show you whence at least a portion of the mephitic compound comes, while the open doorless privies that hang over the water side on one of the banks, and the dark streaks of filth down the walls where the drains from each house discharge themselves into the ditch on the opposite side, tell you how the pollution of the ditch is supplied.

The water is covered with a scum almost like a cobweb, and prismatic with grease. In it float large masses of green rotting weed, and against the posts of the bridges are swollen carcasses of dead animals, almost bursting with the gases of putrefaction. Along its shores are heaps of indescribable filth, the phosphoretted smell from which tells you of the rotting fish there, while the oyster shells are like pieces of slate from their coating of mud and filth. In some parts the fluid is almost as red as blood from the colouring matter that pours into it from the reeking leather-dressers' close by.

The striking peculiarity of Jacob's Island consists in the wooden galleries and sleeping-rooms at the back of the houses which overhang the dark flood, and are built upon piles, so that the place has positively the air of a Flemish street, flanking a sewer instead of a canal; while the little rickety bridges that span the ditches and connect court with court, give it the appearance of the Venice of drains, where channels before and behind the houses do duty for the ocean. Across some parts of the stream whole rooms have been built, so that house adjoins house; and here, with the very stench of death rising through the boards, human beings sleep night after night, until the last sleep of all comes upon them years before its time. Scarce a house but yellow linen is hanging to dry over the balustrade of staves, or else run out on a long oar where the sulphur-coloured clothes hang over the waters, and you are almost wonderstruck to see their form and colour unreflected in the putrid ditch beneath.

At the back of nearly every house that boasts a square foot or two of outlet – and the majority have none at all – are pig-sties. In front waddle ducks, while cocks and hens scratch at the cinderheaps. Indeed the creatures that fatten on offal are the only living things that seem to flourish here

The inhabitants themselves show in their faces the poisonous influence of the mephitic air they breathe. Either their skins are white, like parchment, telling of the impaired digestion, the languid circulation, and the coldness of the skin peculiar to persons suffering from chronic poisoning, or else their cheeks are flushed hectically, and their eyes are glassy, showing the wasting fever and general decline of the bodily functions. The brown, earthlike complexion of some, and their sunk eyes, with the dark areolae round them, tell you that the sulphuretted hydrogen of the atmosphere in which they live has been absorbed into the blood; while others are remarkable for the watery eye exhibiting the increased secretion of tears so peculiar to those who are exposed to the exhalations of hydrosulphate of ammonia.

Scarcely a girl that has not suffusion and soreness of the eyes, so that you would almost fancy she had been swallowing small doses of arsenic; while it is evident from the irritation and discharge from the mucous membranes of the nose and eyes for which all the children are distinguished, that the poor emaciated things are suffering from continual inhalation of the vapour of carbonate of ammonia and other deleterious gases.

Nor was this to be wondered at, when the whole air reeked with the stench of rotting animal and vegetable matter: for the experiment of Professor Donovan has shown that a rabbit, with only its body enclosed in a bladder filled with sulphuretted hydrogen, and allowed to breathe freely, will die in ten minutes. Thénard also has proved that one eight hundredth part of this gas in the atmosphere is sufficient to destroy a dog, and one two hundred and fiftieth will kill a horse; while Mr Taylor, in his book on poisons, assures us that the men who were engaged in excavating the Thames Tunnel suffered severely during the work from the presence of this gas in the atmosphere in which they were obliged to labour. 'The air, as well as the water which trickled through the roof,' he tells us, 'was found to contain sulphuretted hydrogen. This was probably derived from the action of the iron pyrites in the clay. By respiring this atmosphere the strongest and most robust men were, in the course of a few months, reduced to a state of extreme exhaustion and died. They became emaciated, and fell into a state of low fever, accompanied with delirium. In one case which I saw,' he adds, 'the face of the man was pale, the lips of a violet hue, the eyes sunk and dark all round, and the whole muscular system flabby and emaciated'. To give the reader some idea as to the extent with which the air in Jacob's Island is charged with this most deadly compound, it will be sufficient to say that a silver spoon of which we caught sight in one of the least wretched dwellings was positively chocolate-coloured by the action of the sulphur on the metal.

On approaching the tidal ditch from the Neckinger-road, the shutters of the house at the corner were shut from top to bottom. Our intelligent and obliging guide, Dr Martin, informed us that a girl was then lying dead there from cholera, and that but very recently another victim had fallen in the house adjoining it. This was the beginning of the tale of death, for the tidal ditch was filled up to this very point. Here, however, its putrefying waters were left to mingle their poison with the 267 cubic feet of air that each man daily takes into his lungs, and this was the point whence the pestilence commenced its ravages. As we walked down George-row, our informant told us that at the corner of London-street he could see, a short time back, as many as nine houses in which there were one or two persons lying dead of the cholera at the same time; and yet there could not have been more than a dozen tenements visible from the spot.

We crossed the bridge, and spoke to one of the inmates. In answer to our questions, she told us she was never well. Indeed, the signs of the deadly influence of the place were painted in the earthy complexion of the poor woman. 'Neither I nor my children know what health is,' said she. 'But what is one to do? We must live where our bread is. I've tried to let the house, and put a bill up, but cannot get any one to take it.'

From this spot we were led to narrow close courts, where the sun never shone, and the air seemed almost as stagnant and putrid as the ditch we had left. The blanched cheeks of the people that now came out to stare at us, were white as vegetables grown in the dark, and as we stopped to look down the alley, our informant told us that the place teemed with children, and that if a horn was blown they would swarm like bees at the sound of a gong. The houses were mostly inhabited by 'corn-runners', coal-porters, and 'longshore-men', getting a precarious living – earning some times as much as twelve shillings a day, and then for weeks doing nothing. Fevers prevailed in these courts we were told more than at the side of the ditch.

By this way we reached a dismal stack of hovels called, by a strange incongruity, Pleasant-row. Inquiring of one of the inmates, we were informed that they were quite comfortable now! The stench had been all removed, said the woman, and we were invited to pass to the back-yard as evidence of the fact. We did so; the boards bent under our feet, and the air in the cellar-like yard was foetid to positive nausea. As we left the house a child sat nursing a dying half-comatose baby on a door step. The skin of its little arms, instead of being plumped out with health, was loose and shrivelled, like an old crone's, and had a flabby monkey-like appearance more than the character of human cuticle. The almost jaundiced colour of the child's skin, its half paralysed limbs, and state of stupor, told it was suffering from some slow poison; indeed the symptoms might readily have been mistaken for those of chronic poisoning from acetate of lead. At the end of this row our friend informed us that the last house on either side was *never* free from fever.

Continuing our course we reached 'The Folly', another street so narrow that the names and trades of the shopmen were painted on boards that stretched, across the street, from the roof of their own house to that of their neighbour's. We were here stopped by our companion in front of a house 'to let'. The building was as narrow and as unlike a human habitation as the wooden houses in a child's box of toys. 'In this house,' said our friend, 'when the scarlet fever was raging in the neighbourhood, the barber who was living here suffered fearfully from it; and no sooner did the man get well of this than he was seized with typhus, and scarcely had he recovered from the first attack than he was struck down a second time with the same terrible disease. Since then he has lost his child with cholera, and at this moment his wife is in the workhouse suffering from the same affliction. The only wonder is that they are not all dead, for as the man sat at his meals in his small shop, if he put his hand against the wall behind him, it would be covered with the soil of his neighbour's privy, sopping through the wall. At the back of the house was an open sewer, and the privies were full to the seat.'

One fact, says an eminent writer in toxicology, is worthy of the attention of medical jurists, namely, that the respiration of an atmosphere only slightly impregnated with the gases emanating from drains and sewers, may, if long continued, seriously affect an individual and cause death. M. D'Arcet had to examine a lodging in Paris, in which three young and vigorous men had died successively in the course of a few years, under similar symptoms. The lodging consisted of a bedroom with a chimney, and an ill-ventilated ante-room. The pipe of a privy passed down one side of the room, by the head of the bed, and the wall in this part was damp from infiltration. At the time of the examination there was no perceptible smell in the room, though it was small and low. M. D'Arcet attributed the mortality in the lodging to the slow and long-continued action of the emanations from the pipe.

We then journeyed on to London-street, down which the tidal ditch continues its course. In No. 1 of this street the cholera first appeared seventeen years ago, and spread up it with fearful virulence; but this year it appeared at the opposite end, and ran down it with like severity. As we passed along the reeking banks of the sewer the sun shone upon a narrow slip of the water. In the bright light it appeared the colour of strong green tea, and positively looked as solid as black marble in the shadow – indeed it was more like watery mud than muddy water; and yet we were assured this was the only water the wretched inhabitants had to drink. As we gazed in horror at it, we saw drains and sewers emptying their filthy contents into it; we saw a whole tier of doorless privies in the open road, common to men and women, built over it; we heard bucket after bucket of filth splash into it, and the limbs of the vagrant boys bathing in it seemed, by pure force of contrast, white as Parian marble. And yet, as we stood doubting the fearful statement, we saw a little child, from one of the galleries opposite, lower a tin can with a rope to fill a large bucket that stood beside her. In each of the balconies that hung over the stream the self-same tub was to be seen in which the inhabitants put the mucky liquid to stand, so that they may, after it has rested for a day or two, skim the fluid from the solid particles of filth, pollution, and disease. As the little thing dangled her tin cup as gently as possible into the stream, a bucket of night-soil was poured down from the next gallery.

In this wretched place we were taken to a house where an infant lay dead of the cholera. We asked if they *really did* drink the water? The answer was, 'They were obliged to drink the ditch, without they could beg a pailfull or thieve a pailfull of water.' 'But have you spoken to your landlord about having it laid on for you?' 'Yes, sir; and he says he'll do it, and do it, but we know him better than to believe him.' 'Why, sir,' cried another woman, who had shot out from an adjoining room, 'he won't even give us a little whitewash, though we tell him we'll willingly do the work ourselves: and look here, sir,' she added, 'all the tiles have fallen off, and the rain pours in wholesale.'

We had scarcely left the house when a bill caught our eye, announcing that 'this valuable estate' was to be sold!

From this spot we crossed the little shaky bridge into Providence-buildings – a narrow neck of land set in sewers. Here, in front of the houses, were small gardens that a table-cloth would have covered. Still the one dahlia that here raised its round red head made it a happier and brighter place. Never was colour so grateful to the eye. All we had looked at had been so black and dingy, and had smelt so much of churchyard clay, that this little patch of beauty was brighter and greener than ever was oasis in the desert. Here a herd of children came out, and stared at us like sheep. One child our guide singled out from the rest. She had the complexion of tawed leather, and her bright, glassy eyes were sunk so far back in her head, that they looked more like lights shining through the hollow sockets of a skull than a living head, and her bones seemed ready to start through the thin layer of skin. We were told she had had the cholera twice. Her father was dead of it. 'But she, sir,' said a woman addressing us, 'won't die. Ah! if she'd had plenty of victuals and been brought up less hardy she would have been dead and buried long ago, like many more. And here's another,' she added, pushing forward a long thin woman in rusty black.

'Why, I've know'd her eat as much as a quartern loaf at a meal, and you can't fatten her no how.' Upon this there was a laugh, but in the woman's bloodless cheeks and blue lips we saw that she like the rest was wasting away from the influence of the charnel-like atmosphere around her.

The last place we went to was in Joiner's-court, with four wooden houses in it, in which there had lately been as many as five cases of cholera. In front, the poor souls, as if knowing by an instinct that plants were given to purify the atmosphere, had pulled up the paving-stones before their dwellings, and planted a few stocks here and there in the rich black mould beneath. The first house we went to, a wild ragged-headed boy shot out in answer to our knock, and putting his hands across the doorway, stood there to prevent our entrance. Our friend asked whether he could enter, and see the state of the drainage? 'No; t'ain't convenient,' was the answer, given so quickly and sharply, that the lad forced some ugly and uncharitable suspicion upon us. In the next house, the poor inmate was too glad to meet with any one ready to sympathise with her sufferings. We were taken up into a room, where we were told she had positively lived for nine years. The window was within four feet of a high wall, at the foot of which, until very recently, ran the open common sewer. The room was so dark that it was several minutes before we could see anything within it, and there was a smell of must and dry rot that told of damp and imperfect ventilation, and the unnatural size of the pupils of the wretched woman's eyes convinced us how much too long she had dwelt in this gloomy place.

Here, as usual, we heard stories that made one's blood curdle of the cruelty of those from whom they rented the sties called dwellings. They had begged for pure water to be laid on, and the rain to be shut out; and the answer for eighteen years had been, that the lease was just out. 'They knows it's handy for a man's work,' said one and all, 'and that's the reason why they impose on a body.' This, indeed, seems to us to be the great evil. Out of these wretches' health, comfort, and even lives, small capitalists reap a petty independence; and until the poor are rescued from the fangs of these mercenary men, there is but little hope either for their physical or moral welfare.

The extreme lassitude and deficient energy of both body and mind induced by the mephitic vapours they continually inhale leads them – we may say, *forces* them to seek an unnatural stimulus in the gin-shop; indeed, the publicans of Jacob's Island drive even a more profitable trade than the landlords themselves. What wonder, then, since debility is one of the predisposing conditions of cholera, that – even if these stenches of the foul tidal ditch be not the *direct* cause of the disease – that the impaired digestive functions, the languid circulation, the depression of mind produced by the continued inhalation of the noxious gases of the tidal ditch, together with the intemperance that it induces – the cold, damp houses – and, above all, the quenching of the thirst and cooking of the food with water saturated with the very excrements of their fellow creatures, should make Jacob's Island notorious as the Jessore of England.

If Mayhew hadn't been such a disorganised writer, one could imagine that, in this piece, he deliberately decided to feature examples of the type of writing that would characterise the torrent of articles and books he was to produce over the next twenty years about London life.

The vivid metaphor – 'if a horn was blown they would swarm like bees at the sound of a gong'; the pin-sharp observation – 'a silver spoon of which we caught sight in one of the least wretched dwellings was positively chocolate-coloured by the action of the sulphur on the metal'; the personal observation that is effective because it is understated – 'As we gazed in horror at it, we saw drains and sewers emptying their filthy contents into it; we saw a whole tier of doorless privies in the open road, common to men and women, built over it; we heard bucket after bucket of filth splash into it, and the limbs of the vagrant boys bathing in it seemed, by pure force of contrast, white as Parian marble.' The 'marble' here, like the 'chocolate' in the description of the spoon is all the more effective because of the contrast between the usual context of these everyday words and the nightmare scene Mayhew is witnessing.

Then there is the attention to evidence. Mayhew's statements about the connection between disease and the environment are backed by references to scientific research. The observations of Professor Donovan, Thénard, Mr Taylor, and others are paraded before us. Even though they were all wrong about the causes of cholera – to be identified six years later as a bacterium in the water after an outbreak of cholera in Soho – they show Mayhew's concern to justify, sometimes in unnecessary detail, the factual statements he makes.

Time and again, as shown in the extracts featured in the rest of the book, Mayhew's writing treads a sure line between outward objectivity and underlying emotion, and between evidence and opinion, to bring to life the city of London and the people who lived and worked there.

Chapter Two: Streets and Alleyways

Mayhew's descriptions of the streets and houses of the poorer parts of London convey the kind of detail that sums up not just the physical appearance of an environment but the characters of the people who inhabit it. His sharp eyes spot features in the environment that might seem too trivial for someone else to report but which can be more important for understanding the lives of poor Londoners than the enumeration of rooms, stairs, living space or furniture.

In his quest to understand where and how poor people lived, Mayhew had asked one of his informants to take him to a cheap lodging house, often the only accommodation available to people whose earnings were erratic or whose lives were so unstable that they had no permanent place to live. After his first visit, he was so intrigued, he decided to return the following evening and provide a free meal for anyone who would come and answer his questions. As often happens, he leads us, almost by the hand, towards the object of his interest, describing the journey as well as the destination.

The streets were alive with sailors, and bonnetless and capless women. The Jews' shops and public-houses were all open, and parties of 'jolly tars' reeled past us, singing and bawling on their way. Had it not been that here and there a stray shop was closed, it would have been impossible to have guessed it was Sunday. We dived down a narrow court, at the entrance of which lolled Irish labourers smoking short pipes. Across the court hung lines, from which dangled dirty-white clothes to dry; and as we walked on, ragged, unwashed, shoeless children scampered past us, chasing one another. At length we reached a large open yard. In the centre of it stood several empty costermongers' trucks and turned-up carts, with their shafts high in the air. At the bottom of these lay two young girls huddled together, asleep. Their bare heads told their mode of life, while it was evident, from their muddy Adelaide boots, that they had walked the streets all night. My companion tried to see if he knew them, but they slept too soundly to be roused by gentle means. We passed on, and a few paces further on there sat grouped on a door-step four women, of the same character as the last two. One had her head covered up in an old brown shawl, and was sleeping in the lap of the one next to her. The other two were eating walnuts; and a coarse-featured man in knee breeches and 'ankle-jacks' was stretched on the ground close beside them.

At length we reached the lodging-house. It was night when I had first visited the place, and all now was new to me. The entrance was through a pair of large green gates, which gave it somewhat the appearance of a stable yard. Over the kitchen door there hung a clothes-line, on which were a wet shirt and a pair of ragged canvas trousers, brown with tar. Entering the kitchen, we found it so full of smoke that the sun's rays, which shot slanting down through a broken tile in the roof, looked like a shaft of light cut through the fog. The flue of the chimney stood out from the bare brick wall like a buttress, and was black all the way up with the smoke; the beams, which hung down from the roof, and ran from wall to wall, were of the same colour; and in the centre, to light the room, was a rude iron gas-pipe, such as are used at night when the streets are turned up. The floor was unboarded, and a wooden seat projected from the wall all round the room. In front of this was ranged a series of tables, on which lolled dozing men. A number of the inmates were grouped around the fire; some kneeling toasting herrings, of which the place smelt strongly; others, without shirts, seated on the ground close beside it for warmth; and others drying the ends of cigars they had picked up in the streets. As we entered the men rose, and never was so motley and so ragged an assemblage seen. Their hair was matted like flocks of wool, and their chins were grimy with their unshorn beards. Some were in dirty smock-frocks; others in old red plush waistcoats, with long sleeves. One was dressed in an old shooting-jacket, with large wooden buttons; a second in a blue flannel sailor's shirt; and a third, a mere boy, wore a long camlet coat reaching to his heels, and with the ends of the sleeves hanging over his hands. The features of the lodgers wore every kind of expression: one lad was positively handsome, and there was a frankness in his face and a straightforward look in his eye that strongly impressed me with a sense of his honesty, even although I was assured he was a confirmed pickpocket. The young thief who had brought back the elevenpence halfpenny change out of the shilling that had been entrusted to him on the preceding evening, was far from prepossessing, now that I could see him better.* His cheek-bones were high, while his hair, cut close on the top, with a valance of locks, as it were, left hanging in front, made me look upon him with no slight suspicion. On the form at the end of the kitchen was one whose squalor and wretchedness produced a feeling approaching to awe. His eyes were sunk deep in his head, his cheeks were drawn in, and his nostrils pinched with evident want, while his dark stubbly beard gave a grimness to his appearance that was almost demoniac; and yet there was a patience in his look that was almost pitiable. His clothes were black and shiny at every fold with grease, and his coarse shirt was so brown with long wearing, that it was only with close inspection you could see that it had once been a checked one: on his feet he had a pair of lady's side-laced boots, the toes of which had been cut off so that he might get them on. I never beheld so gaunt a picture of famine. To this day the figure of the man haunts me.

* See Chapter Ten: 'Our Pet Thief'

The dinner had been provided for thirty, but the news of the treat had spread, and there was a muster of fifty. We hardly knew how to act. It was, however, left to those whose names had been taken down as being present on the previous evening to say what should be done; and the answer from one and all was that the new-comers were to share the feast with them. The dinner was then half-portioned out in an adjoining outhouse into twenty-five platefuls – the entire stock of crockery belonging to the establishment numbering no more – and afterwards handed into the kitchen through a small window to each party, as his name was called out. As he hurried to the seat behind the bare table, he commenced tearing the meat asunder with his fingers, for knives and forks were unknown there. Some, it is true, used bits of wood like skewers, but this seemed almost like affectation in such a place: others sat on the ground with the plate of meat and pudding on their laps; while the beggar-boy, immediately on receiving his portion, danced along the room, whirling the plate round on his thumb as he went, and then, dipping his nose in the plate, seized a potato in his mouth. I must confess the sight of the hungry crowd gnawing their food was far from pleasant to contemplate; so, while the dinner was being discussed, I sought to learn from those who remained to be helped, how they had fallen to so degraded a state. A sailor lad assured me he had been robbed of his mariner's ticket; that he could not procure another under thirteen shillings; and not having as many pence, he was unable to obtain another ship. What could he do? he said. He knew no trade: he could only get employment occasionally as a labourer at the docks; and this was so seldom, that if it had not been for the few things he had, he must have starved outright. The good-looking youth I have before spoken of wanted but three pounds ten shillings to get back to America. He had worked his passage over here; had fallen into bad company; been imprisoned three times for picking pockets; and was heartily wearied of his present course. He could get no work. In America he would be happy, and among his friends again. I spoke to the gentleman who had brought me to the spot, and who knew them all well. His answers, however, gave me little hope. The boy, whose face seemed beaming with innate frankness and honesty, had been apprenticed by him to a shoe-stitcher. But, no! he preferred vagrancy to work. I could have sworn he was a trustworthy lad, and shall never believe in 'looks' again.

The dinner finished, I told the men assembled there that I should come some evening in the course of the week, and endeavour to ascertain from them some definite information concerning the persons usually frequenting such houses as theirs. On our way home, my friend recognised, among the females we had before seen huddled on the step outside the lodging-house, a young woman whom he had striven to get back to her parents. Her father had been written to, and would gladly receive her. Again the girl was exhorted to leave her present companions and return home. The tears streamed from her eyes at mention of her mother's name; but she would not stir. Her excuse was, that she had no clothes proper to go in. Her father and mother were very respectable, she said, and she could not go back to them as she was. It was evident, by her language, she had at least been well educated. She would not listen, however, to my friend's exhortations; so, seeing that his entreaties were wasted upon her, we left her, and wended our way home.

[...]

The lodging-house[...]makes up as many as eighty-four 'bunks', or beds, for which twopence per night is charged. For this sum the parties lodging there for the night are entitled to the use of the kitchen for the following day. In this a fire is kept all day long, at which they are allowed to cook their food. The kitchen opens at five in the morning, and closes at about eleven at night, after which hour no fresh lodger is taken in, and all those who slept in the house the night before, but who have not sufficient money to pay for their bed at that time, are turned out. Strangers who arrive in the course of the day must procure a tin ticket, by paying twopence at the wicket in the office, previously to being allowed to enter the kitchen. The kitchen is about forty feet long by about forty wide. The 'bunks' are each about seven feet long, and one foot ten inches wide, and the grating on which the straw mattress is placed is about twelve inches from the ground. The wooden partitions between the 'bunks' are about four feet high. The coverings are a leather or a rug, but leathers are generally preferred. Of these 'bunks' there are five rows, of about twenty-four deep; two rows being placed head to head, with a gangway between each of such two rows, and the other row against the wall. The average number of persons sleeping in this house of a night is sixty. Of these there are generally about thirty pickpockets, ten street beggars, a few infirm old people who subsist occasionally upon parish relief and occasionally upon charity, ten or fifteen dock-labourers, about the same number of low and precarious callings, such as the neighbourhood affords, and a few persons who have been in good circumstances, but who have been reduced from a variety of causes. At one time there were as many as nine persons lodging in this house who subsisted by picking up dogs' dung out of the streets, getting about five shillings for every basketful. The earnings of one of these men were known to average nine shillings per week. There are generally lodging in the house a few bone-grubbers, who pick up bones, rags, iron, &c., out of the streets. Their average earnings are about a shilling per day. There are several mud-larks, or youths who go down to the water-side when the tide is out, to see whether any article of value has been left upon the bank of the river. The person supplying this information to me, who was for some time resident in the house, has seen brought home by these persons a drum of figs at one time, and a Dutch cheese at another. These were sold in small lots or slices to the other lodgers.

The pickpockets generally lodging in the house consist of handkerchief-stealers, shoplifters – including those who rob the till as well as steal articles from the doors of shops. Legs and breasts of mutton are frequently brought in by this class of persons. There are seldom any housebreakers lodging in such places, because they require a room of their own, and mostly live with prostitutes. Besides pickpockets, there are also lodging in the house speculators in stolen goods. These may be dock-labourers or Billingsgate porters, having a few shillings in their pockets. With these they purchase the booty of the juvenile thieves. 'I have known,' says my informant, 'these speculators wait in the kitchen, walking about with their hands in their pockets, till a little fellow would come in with such a thing as a cap, a piece of bacon, or a piece of mutton. They would purchase it, and then either retail it amongst the other lodgers in the kitchen or take it to some "fence", where they would receive a profit upon it.' The general feeling of the kitchen – excepting with four or five individuals – is to encourage theft. The encouragement to the 'gonaff', (a Hebrew word signifying a young thief, probably learnt from the Jew 'fences' in the neighbourhood) consists in laughing at and applauding his dexterity in thieving; and whenever anything is brought in, the 'gonaff' is greeted for his good luck, and a general rush is made towards him to see the produce of his thievery. The 'gonaffs' are generally young boys; about twenty out of thirty of these lads are under twenty-one years of age. They almost all of them love idleness, and will only work for one or two days together, but then they will work very hard. It is a singular fact that, as a body, the pickpockets are generally very sparing of drink. They are mostly libidinous, indeed universally so, and spend whatever money they can spare upon the low prostitutes round about the neighbourhood. Burglars and smashers generally rank above this class of thieves. A burglar would not condescend to sit among pickpockets. My informant has known a housebreaker to say with a sneer, when requested to sit down with the 'gonaffs', 'No, no! I may be a thief, sir; but, thank God, at least I'm a respectable one.' The beggars who frequent these houses go about different markets and streets asking charity of the people that pass by. They generally go out in couples; the business of one of the two being to look out and give warning when the policeman is approaching, and of the other to stand 'shallow'; that is to say, to stand with very little clothing on, shivering and shaking, sometimes with bandages round his legs, and sometimes with his arm in a sling. Others beg 'scran' (broken victuals) of the servants at respectable houses, and bring it home to the lodging-house, where they sell it. You may see, I am told, the men who lodge in the place, and obtain an honest living, watch for these beggars coming in, as if they were the best victuals in the city. My informant knew an instance of a lad who seemed to be a very fine little fellow, and promised to have been possessed of excellent mental capabilities if properly directed, who came to the lodging-house when out of a situation as an errand-boy. He stayed there a month or six weeks, during which time he was tampered with by the others, and ultimately became a confirmed 'gonaff'. The conversation among the lodgers relates chiefly to thieving and the best manner of stealing. By way of practice, a boy will often pick the pocket of one of the lodgers walking about the room, and if detected declare he did not mean it.

The sanitary state of these houses is very bad. Not only do the lodgers generally swarm with vermin, but there is little or no ventilation to the sleeping-rooms, in which sixty persons, of the foulest habits, usually sleep every night. There are no proper washing utensils, neither towels nor basins, nor wooden bowls. There are one or two buckets, but these are not meant for the use of the lodgers, but for cleaning the rooms. The lodgers never think of washing themselves. The cleanliest among them will do so in the bucket, and then wipe themselves with their pocket-handkerchiefs, or the tails of their shirts.[7]

When his canvas is larger than a court or lodging house, as in the following description of the London docks, Mayhew's observations still include details that others might miss and which bring to life a piece of writing which in other hands might end up as a bland and solely factual account. Typical of this is the shops selling mariners' compasses 'with their cards trembling with the motion of the cabs and waggons passing in the street'. But the facts are still important, and Mayhew starts this piece with some vital statistics.

The London Dock occupies an area of ninety acres, and is situated in the three parishes of St George, Shadwell, and Wapping. The population of those three parishes in 1841 was 55,500, and the number of inhabited houses 8,000, which covered a space equal to 338 acres. This is in the proportion of twenty-three inhabited houses to an acre and seven individuals to each house. The number of persons to each inhabited house is, despite of the crowded lodging-houses with which it abounds, not beyond the average for all London. I have already shown that Bethnal-green, which is said to possess the greatest number of low-rented houses, had only, upon an average, seventeen inhabited houses to each acre, while the average through London was but 5.5 houses per acre. So that it appears that in the three parishes of St George's-in-the-East, Shadwell, and Wapping, the houses are more than four times more crowded than in the other parts of London, and more numerous by half as many again than those even in the low-rented district of Bethnal-green. This affords us a good criterion as to the character of the neighbourhood, and, consequently, of the people living in the vicinity of the London Dock.

The courts and alleys round about the dock swarm with low lodging-houses; and are inhabited either by the dock-labourers, sackmakers, watermen, or that peculiar class of the London poor who pick up a living by the water-side. The open streets themselves have all more or less a maritime character. Every other shop is either stocked with gear for the ship or for the sailor. The windows of one house are filled with quadrants and bright brass sextants, chronometers, and huge mariners' compasses, with their cards trembling with the motion of the cabs and wagons passing in the street. Then comes the sailors' cheap shoe-mart, rejoicing in the attractive sign of 'Jack and his Mother'. Every public-house is a 'Jolly Tar', or something equally taking. Then come sailmakers, their windows stowed with ropes and lines smelling of tar. All the grocers are provision-agents, and exhibit in their windows the cases of meat and biscuits; and every article is warranted to keep in any climate. The corners of the streets, too, are mostly monopolised by slopsellers; their windows parti-coloured with bright red-and-blue flannel shirts; the doors nearly blocked up with hammocks and 'well-oiled nor'westers'; and the front of the house itself nearly covered with canvas trousers, rough pilot-coats, and shiny black dreadnoughts. The passengers alone would tell you that you were in the maritime districts of London. Now you meet a satin-waistcoated mate, or a black sailor with his large fur cap, or else a Custom-house officer in his brass-buttoned jacket.

The London Dock can accommodate 500 ships, and the ware-houses will contain 232,000 tons of goods. The entire struc-ture cost £4,000,000 in money: the tobacco warehouses alone cover five acres of ground. The wall surrounding the dock cost £65,000. One of the wine-vaults has an area of seven acres, and in the whole of them there is room for stowing 60,000 pipes of wine. The warehouses round the wharfs are exposing from their extent, but are much less lofty than those at St Katherine's; and being situated at some distance from the dock, goods cannot be craned out of the ship's hold and stowed away at one operation. According to the last half-yearly report, the number of ships which entered the dock during the six months ending the 31st of May last was 704, measuring upwards of 195,000 tons. The amount of earnings during that period was £230,000 and odd, and the amount of expenditure nearly £121,000. The stock of goods in the warehouses last May was upwards of 170,000 tons.

As you enter the dock the sight of the forest of masts in the distance, and the tall chimneys vomiting clouds of black smoke, and the many coloured flags flying in the air, has a most peculiar effect; while the sheds with the monster wheels arching through the roofs look like the paddle-boxes of huge steamers. Along the quay you see, now men with their faces blue with indigo, and now gaugers, with their long brass-tipped rule dripping with spirit from the cask they have been probing. Then will come a group of flaxen-haired sailors chattering German; and next a black sailor, with a cotton handkerchief twisted turban-like round his head. Presently a blue-smocked butcher, with fresh meat and a bunch of cabbages in the tray on his shoulder; and shortly afterwards a mate, with green paroquets in a wooden cage. Here you will see sitting on a bench a sorrowful-looking woman, with new bright cooking tins at her feet, telling you she is an emigrant preparing for her voyage. As you pass along this quay the air is pungent with tobacco; on that it overpowers you with the fumes of rum; then you are nearly sickened with the stench of hides, and huge bins of horns; and shortly afterwards the atmosphere is fragrant with coffee and spice. Nearly every-where you meet stacks of cork, or else yellow bins of sulphur, or lead-coloured copper-ore. As you enter this warehouse, the flooring is sticky, as if it had been newly tarred, with the sugar that has leaked through the casks; and as you descend into the dark vaults, you see long lines of lights hanging from the black arches, and lamps flitting about midway. Here you sniff the fumes of the wine, and there the peculiar fungus-smell of dry rot; then the jumble of sounds as you pass along the dock blends in anything but sweet concord. The sailors are singing boisterous nigger songs from the Yankee ship just entering; the cooper is hammering at the casks on the quay; the chains of the cranes, loosed of their weight, rattle as they fly up again; the ropes splash in the water; some captain shouts his orders through his hands; a goat bleats from some ship in the basin; and empty casks roll along the stones with a heavy drum-like sound. Here the heavily-laden ships are down far below the quay, and you descend to them by ladders; whilst in another basin they are high up out of the water, so that their green copper sheathing is almost level with the eye of the passenger; while above his head a long line of bowsprits stretches far over the quay; and from them hang spars and planks as a gangway to each ship.

This immense establishment is worked by from one to three thousand hands, according as the business is either brisk or slack. Out of this number there are always 400 to 500 permanent labourers, receiving on an average sixteen shillings and sixpence per week, with the exception of coopers, carpenters, smiths, and other mechanics, who are paid the usual wages of those crafts. Besides these are many hundred – from 1,000 to 2,500 – casual labourers, who are engaged at the rate of two and sixpence per day in the summer and two and fourpence in the winter months. Frequently, in case of many arrivals, extra hands are hired in the course of the day, at the rate of fourpence per hour. For the permanent labourers a recommendation is required; but for the casual labourers no character is demanded. The number of the casual hands engaged by the day depends, of course, upon the amount of work to be done; and I find that the total number of labourers in the dock varies from 500 to 3,000 and odd. On the 4th May, 1849, the number of hands engaged, both permanent and casual, was 2,794; on the 26th of the same month it was 3,012; and on the 30th it was 1,189. These appear to be the extreme of the variation for that year: the fluctuation is due to a greater or lesser number of ships entering the dock. The lowest number of ships entering the dock in any one week last year was twenty-nine, while the highest number was 141. This rise and fall is owing to the prevalence of easterly winds, which serve to keep the ships back, and so make the business slack. Now, deducting the lowest number of hands employed from the highest number, we have no less than 1,823 individuals who obtain so precarious a subsistence by their labour at the docks, that by the mere shifting of the wind they may be all deprived of their daily bread. Calculating the wages at two and sixpence per day for each, the company would have paid £376 and ten shillings to the 3,012 hands employed on the 26th of May 1849; while only £148 twelve shillings and sixpence would have been paid to the 1,189 hands engaged on the 30th of the same month. Hence, not only would 1,823 hands have been thrown out of employ by the chopping of the wind, but the labouring men dependent upon the business of the docks for their subsistence would in one day have been deprived of £227 seventeen shillings and sixpence. This will afford the reader some faint idea of the precarious character of the subsistence obtained by the labourers employed in this neighbourhood, and, consequently, as it has been well proved, that all men who obtain their livelihood by irregular employment are the most intemperate and improvident of all.

It will be easy to judge what may be the condition and morals of a class who today, as a body, may earn near upon £400, and tomorrow only £150. I had hoped to have been able to have shown the fluctuations in the total amount of wages paid to the dock-labourers for each week throughout the whole year; and so, by contrasting the comparative affluence and comfort of one week with the distress and misery of the other, to have afforded the reader some more vivid idea of the body of men who are performing, perhaps, the heaviest labour, and getting the most fickle provision of all. But still I will endeavour to impress him with some faint idea of the struggle there is to gain the uncertain daily bread. Until I saw with my own eyes this scene of greedy despair, I could not have believed that there was so mad an eagerness to work, and so biting a want of it, among so vast a body of men. A day or two before I had sat at midnight in the room of the starving weaver; and as I heard him tell his bitter story, there was a patience in his misery that gave it more an air of heroism than desperation. But in the scenes I have lately witnessed the want has been positively tragic, and the struggle for life partaking of the sublime. The reader must first remember what kind of men the casual labourers generally are. They are men, it should be borne in mind, who are shut out from the usual means of life by the want of character. Hence, you are not astonished to hear from those who are best acquainted with the men, that there are hundreds among the body who are known thieves, and who go to the docks to seek a living; so that, if taken for any past offence, their late industry may plead for some little lenity in their punishment.

He who wishes to behold one of the most extraordinary and least-known scenes of this metropolis, should wend his way to the London Dock gates at half-past seven in the morning. There he will see congregated within the principal entrance masses of men of all grades, looks, and kinds. Some in half-fashioned surtouts burst at the elbows, with the dirty shirts showing through. Others in greasy sporting jackets, with red pimpled faces. Others in the rags of their half-slang gentility, with the velvet collars of their paletots worn through to the canvas. Some in rusty black, with their waistcoats fastened tight up to the throat. Others, again, with the knowing thieves' curl on each side of the jaunty cap; whilst here and there you may see a big-whiskered Pole, with his hands in the pockets of his plaited French trousers. Some loll outside the gates, smoking the pipe which is forbidden within; but these are mostly Irish.

Presently you know, by the stream pouring through the gates and the rush towards particular spots, that the 'calling foremen' have made their appearance. Then begins the scuffling and scrambling forth of countless hands high in the air, to catch the eye of him whose voice may give them work. As the foreman calls from a book the names, some men jump up on the backs of the others, so as to lift themselves high above the rest, and attract the notice of him who hires them. All are shouting. Some cry aloud his surname, some his Christian name, others call out their own names, to remind him that they are there. Now the appeal is made in Irish blarney – now in broken English. Indeed, it is a sight to sadden the most callous, to see thousands of men struggling for only one day's hire; the scuffle being made the fiercer by the knowledge that hundreds out of the number there assembled must be left to idle the day out in want. To look in the faces of that hungry crowd is to see a sight that must be ever remembered. Some are smiling to the foreman to coax him into remembrance of them; others, with their protruding eyes, eager to snatch at the hoped-for pass. For weeks many have gone there, and gone through the same struggle – the same cries; and have gone away, after all, without the work they had screamed for.

From this it might be imagined that the work was of a peculiarly light and pleasant kind, and so, when I first saw the scene, I could not help imagining myself. But, in reality, the labour is of that heavy and continuous character that you would fancy only the best fed could stand it. The work may be divided into three classes. 1. Wheel-work, or that which is moved by the muscles of the legs and weight of the body; 2. jigger, or winch-work, or that which is moved by the muscles of the arm. In each of these the labourer is stationary; but in the truck work, which forms the third class, the labourer has to travel over a space of ground greater or less in proportion to the distance which the goods have to be removed.

The wheel-work is performed somewhat on the system of the treadwheel, with the exception that the force is applied inside instead of outside the wheel. From six to eight men enter a wooden cylinder or drum, upon which are nailed battens, and the men laying hold of ropes commence treading the wheel round, occasionally singing the while, and stamping time in a manner that is pleasant, from its novelty. The wheel is generally about sixteen feet in diameter and eight to nine feet broad; and the six or eight men treading within it, will lift from sixteen to eighteen hundred weight, and often a ton, forty times in an hour, an average of twenty-seven feet high. Other men will get out a cargo of from 800 to 900 casks of wine, each cask averaging about five hundred weight, and being lifted about eighteen feet, in a day and a half. At trucking each man is said to go on an average thirty miles a-day, and two-thirds of that time he is moving one and a half hundred weight at six miles and a-half per hour.

This labour, though requiring to be seen to be properly understood, must still appear so arduous that one would imagine it was not of that tempting nature, that 3,000 men could be found every day in London desperate enough to fight and battle for the privilege of getting two and sixpence by it; and even if they fail in 'getting taken on' at the commencement of the day, that they should then retire to the appointed yard, there to remain hour after hour in the hope that the wind might blow them some stray ship, so that other gangs might be wanted, and the calling foreman seek them there. It is a curious sight to see the men waiting in these yards to be hired at fourpence per hour, for such are the terms given in the after part of the day. There, seated on long benches ranged against the wall, they remain, some telling their miseries and some their crimes to one another, whilst others doze away their time. Rain or sunshine, there can always be found plenty ready to catch the stray shilling or eightpence worth of work. By the size of the shed you can tell how many men sometimes remain there in the pouring rain, rather than run the chance of losing the stray hours' work. Some loiter on the bridges close by, and presently, as their practised eye or ear tells them that the calling foreman is in want of another gang, they rush forward in a stream towards the gate, though only six or eight at most can be hired out of the hundred or more that are waiting there. Again the same mad fight takes place as in the morning. There is the same jumping on benches, the same raising of hands, the same entreaties, and the same failure as before. It is strange to mark the change that takes place in the manner of the men when the foreman has left. Those that have been engaged go smiling to their labour. Indeed, I myself met on the quay just such a chuckling gang passing to their work. Those who are left behind give vent to their disappointment in abuse of him whom they had been supplicating and smiling at a few minutes before. Upon talking with some of the unsuccessful ones, they assured me that the men who had supplanted them had only gained their ends by bribing the foreman who had engaged them. This I made a point of inquiring into, and the deputy-warehousekeeper, of whom I sought the information, soon assured me, by the production of his book, that he himself was the person who chose the men, the foreman merely executing his orders: and this, indeed, I found to be the custom throughout the dock.

At four o'clock the eight hours' labour ceases, and then comes the paying. The names of the men are called out of the muster-book, and each man, as he answers to the cry, has half-a-crown given to him. So rapidly is this done that, in a quarter of an hour, the whole of the men have had their wages paid them. They then pour towards the gate. Here two constables stand, and as each man passes through the wicket, he takes his hat off, and is felt from head to foot by the dock-officers and attendant: and yet, with all the want, misery, and temptation, the millions of pounds of property amid which they work, and the thousands of pipes and hogsheads of wines and spirits about the docks, I am informed, upon the best authority, that there are on an average but thirty charges of drunkenness in the course of the year, and only eight of dishonesty every month. This may, perhaps, arise from the vigilance of the superintendents; but to see the distressed condition of the men who seek and gain employment in the London Dock, it appears almost incredible, that out of so vast a body of men, without means and without character, there should be so little vice or crime. There still remains one curious circumstance to be added in connexion with the destitution of the dock-labourers. Close to the gate by which they are obliged to leave, sits on a coping-stone the refreshment man, with his two large canvas pockets tied in front of him, and filled with silver and copper, ready to give change to those whom he has trusted with their dinner that day until they were paid.

As the men passed slowly on in a double file towards the gate, I sat beside the victualler, and asked him what constituted the general dinner of the labourers. He told me that he supplied them with pea-soup, bread and cheese, saveloys, and beer. 'Some,' he said, 'had twice as much as others. Some had a pennyworth, some had eatables and a pint of beer; others, two pints, and others four, and some spend their whole half-crown in eating and drinking.' This gave me a more clear insight into the destitution of the men who stood there each morning. Many of them, it was clear, came to the gate without the means of a day's meal, and, being hired, were obliged to go on credit for the very food they worked upon. What wonder, then, that the calling foreman should be often carried many yards away by the struggle and rush of the men around him seeking employment at his hands! One gentleman assured me that he had been taken off his feet and hurried a distance of a quarter of a mile by the eagerness of the impatient crowd around him. [8]

Lodged in the heart of this description of the London dock is a classic piece of Mayhew descriptive writing in which each of the senses, even touch, is used to evoke the experience of actually being there, providing an experience which is as vivid to read today as it must have been to experience 160 years ago. The piece begins with vision – 'As you enter the dock, the sight of the forest of masts…' goes on to smell – 'the air is pungent…sickened with the stench... the atmosphere is fragrant...' – then touch – 'the floor is sticky...' – and then sound – 'the sailors are singing... the cooper is hammering...the ropes splash... some captain shouts... a goat bleats...'

Whether or not this parade of the senses is intentionally comprehensive, its cumulative effect is all the more effective because we know it is based on personal experience.

Chapter Three: Tradecraft

Mayhew's interest in the people he met was voracious. Because his questioning was not always systematic or organised, he would be led into the most arcane areas of people's lives and would pick up the thread of any intriguing aspect of what they told him, and pursue it until he had sucked that topic dry. What you could call 'tradecraft' cropped up time and again in his conversations with tradespeople. From the poorest flower seller to the more prosperous (relatively speaking) tradesman, each person had his or her own wrinkle, a way of doing things that it would be hoped would give the seller an edge over others in a similar line of trade.

'Window dressing' a tray of goods

The itinerant trader carries a tray, and in no few cases, as respects the 'display' of his wares, emulates the tradesman's zeal in 'dressing' a window temptingly. The tray most in use is painted, or mahogany, with 'ledges', front and sides; or, as one man described it, 'an upright four-inch bordering, to keep things in their places'. The back of the tray, which rests against the bearer's breast, is about twelve inches high. Narrow pink tapes are generally attached to the 'ledges' and back, within which are 'slipped' the articles for sale. At the bottom of the tray are often divisions, in which are deposited steel pens, wafers, wax, pencils, pen-holders, and, as one stationer expressed it, 'packable things that you can't get much show out of'. One man – who rather plumed himself on being a thorough master of his trade – said to me:

It's a grand point to display, sir. Now, just take it in this way. Suppose you yourself, sir, lived in my round. Werry good. You hear me cry as I'm approaching your door, and suppose you was a customer, you says to yourself: 'Here's Penny-a-quire,' as I'm called oft enough. And I'll soon be with you, and I gives a extra emphasis at a customer's door. Werry good, you buys the note. *As* you buys the note, you gives a look over my tray, and then you says, 'O, I want some steel pens, and is your ink good?' and you buys some. But for the 'display' you'd have sent to the shopkeeper's, and I should have lost custom, 'cause it wouldn't have struck you.[9]

'Only sell what you know'

One elderly man, long familiar with this branch of the street-trade, [metal articles] expressed to me his conviction that when a mechanic sought his livelihood in the streets, he naturally 'gave his mind to sell what he understood. Now, in my own case,' continued my informant,

I was born and bred a tinman, and when I was driven to a street-life, I never thought of selling anything but tins. How could I, if I wished to do the thing square and proper? – it would be like trying to speak another language. If I'd started on slippers – and I knew a poor man who was set up in the streets by a charitable lady on a stock of gentlemen's slippers – what could I have done? Why, no better than he told me he did. He was a potter down at Deptford, and knew of nothing but flower-pots, and honey-jars for grocers, and them red sorts of pottery. Poor fellow, he might have died of hunger, only the cholera came quickest. But when I'm questioned about my tins, I'm my own man; and it's a great thing, I'm satisfied, in a street-trade, when there's so many cheap shops, and the police and all again you, to understand the goods you're talking about.[10]

Walking-stick seller

The walking-sticks sold in the streets of London are principally purchased at wholesale houses in Mint-street and Union-street, Borough, and their neighbourhoods. 'There's no street-trade,' said an intelligent man, 'and I've tried most that's been, or promised to be, a living in the streets, that is so tiresome as the walking-stick trade. There is nothing in which people are so particular. The stick's sure to be either too short or too long, or too thick or too thin, or too limp or too stiff. You would think it was a simple thing for a man to choose a stick out of a lot, but if you were with me a selling on a fine Sunday at Battersea Fields, you'd see it wasn't. O, it's a tiresome job.'

This trade – like others where the article sold is not of general consumption or primary usefulness – affords, what I once heard a street-seller call, 'a good range'. There is no generally recognised price or value, so that a smart trader in sticks can apportion his offers, or his charges, to what he may think to be the extent of endurance in a customer. What might be twopence to a man who 'looked knowing', might be sixpence to a man who 'looked green'. The common sticks, which are the 'cripples', I was told, of all the sorts of sticks (the spoiled or inferior sticks) mixed with 'common pines', are fifteen pence the dozen. From this price there is a gradual scale up to eight shillings the dozen for 'good polished'; beyond that price the street-seller rarely ventures, and seldom buys even at that (for street-trade) high rate, as fourpenny and sixpenny sticks go off the best; these saleable sticks are generally polished hazel or pine.[11]

Selling muffins

A sharp London lad of fourteen, whose father had been a journeyman baker, and whose mother (a widow) kept a small chandler's shop, gave me the following account:

I turns out with muffins and crumpets, sir, in October, and continues until it gets well into the spring, according to the weather. I carries a fust-rate article; werry much so. If you was to taste 'em, sir, you'd say the same. If I sells three dozen muffins at a ha'penny each, and twice that in crumpets, it's a werry fair day, werry fair; all beyond that is a *good* day. The profit on the three dozen and the others is a shilling, but that's a great help, really a wonderful help, to mother, for I should be only mindin' the shop at home. Perhaps I clears four shillings a week, perhaps more, perhaps less; but that's about it, sir. Some does far better than that, and some can't hold a candle to it. If I has a hextra day's sale, mother'll give me threepence to go to the play, and that hencourages a young man, you know, sir. If there's any unsold, a coffee-shop gets them cheap, and puts 'em off cheap again next morning. My best customers is genteel houses, 'cause I sells a genteel thing. I likes wet days best, 'cause there's werry respectable ladies what don't keep a servant, and they buys to save themselves going out. We're a great conwenience to the ladies, sir – a great conwenience to them as likes a slap-up tea. I *have* made one shilling and eightpence in a day; that was my best. I once took only twopence halfpenny – I don't know why – that was my worst.[12]

Harness maker

I served my time, sir; my relations put me – for my parents died when I was a boy – to a harness furniture maker, in Wa'sall [Walsall], who supplied Mr Dixon, a saddler's iron-monger, in a good way. I had fair makings, and was well treated, and when I was out of my time I worked for another master, and I then found I could make my pad territs [the round loops of the harness pad, through which the reins are passed], my hooks, my buckles, my ornaments (some of 'em crests), as well as any man. I worked only in brass, never plated, but sometimes the body for plating, and mostly territs and hooks. [...] Now I get an odd job with my master some-times, and at others sell my collars, and chains, and key-rings, and locks, and such like. I'm ashamed of the dog-collar locks; I can buy them at twopence a dozen, or one and sixpence a gross; they're sad rubbish. In two or three weeks sometimes, the wire hasp is worn through, just by the rattling of the collar, and the lock falls off.[13]

Crabs and lobsters

There's a great call for haporths and pennorths of lobster or crab, by children; that's their claws. I bile [boil] them all myself, and buy them alive. I can bile twenty in half an hour, and do it over a grate in a back-yard. Lobsters don't fight or struggle much in the hot water, if they're properly packed. It's very few that knows how to bile a lobster as he should be biled. I wish I knew any way of killing lobsters before biling them. I can't kill them without smashing them to bits, and that won't do at all. I kill my crabs before I bile them. I stick them in the throat with a knife and they're dead in an instant.

Some sticks them with a skewer, but they kick a good while with the skewer in them. It's a shame to torture anything when it can be helped. If I didn't kill the crabs they'd shed every leg in the hot water; they'd come out as bare of claws as this plate. I've known it oft enough, as it is; though I kill them uncommon quick, a crab will be quicker and shed every leg -throw them off in the moment I kill them, but that doesn't happen once in fifty times.[14]

Saw-seller

Eight year ago I thought I would try saw-selling: a shop-keeper advised me, and I began on six salt saws, which I sold to oilmen. They're for cutting salt only, and are made of zinc, as steel would rust and dirty the salt. The trade was far better at first than it is now. In good weeks I earned sixteen to eighteen shillings. In bad weeks, ten or twelve shillings. Now I may earn ten shillings, not more, a week, pretty regular: yesterday I made only sixpence. Oilmen are better customers than chance street-buyers, for I'm known to them. There's only one man besides myself selling nothing but saws. I walk, I believe, a hundred miles every week, and that I couldn't do, I know, if I wasn't teetotal. I never long for a taste of liquor if I'm ever so cold or tired. It's all poisonous.

The saws sold are 8 inch, which cost at the swag-shops eight shillings and eight and sixpence a dozen; 10 inch, nine shillings and nine and sixpence; and so on, the price advancing according to the increased size, to 18 inch, thirteen shillings and sixpence the dozen. Larger sizes are seldom sold in the streets.[15]

Of turf-cutting and selling

A man long familiar with this trade, and who knew almost every member of it individually, counted for me thirty-six turf-cutters, to his own knowledge, and was confident that there were forty turf-cutters and sixty sellers in London; the addition of the sellers, however, is but that of ten women, who assist their husbands or fathers in the street sales, – but no women cut turf, – and of ten men who sell, but buy of the cutters.

The turf is simply a sod, but it is considered indispensable that it should contain the leaves of the 'small Dutch clover', (the shamrock of the Irish), the most common of all the trefoils. The turf is used almost entirely for the food and roosting-place of the caged sky-larks. Indeed, one turf-cutter said to me: 'It's only people that don't understand it that gives turf to other birds, but of course if we're asked about it, we say it's good for every bird, pigeons and chickens and all; and very likely it is if they choose to have it.' The principal places for the cutting of turf are at present Shepherd's Bush, Notting Hill, the Caledonian Road, Hampstead, Highgate, Hornsey, Peckham, and Battersea. Chalk Farm was an excellent place, but it is now exhausted, 'fairly flayed' of the shamrocks. Parts of Camden Town were also fertile in turf, but they have been built over. Hackney was a district to which the turf-cutters resorted, but they are now forbidden to cut sods there. Hampstead Heath used to be another harvest-field for these turf-purveyors, but they are now prohibited from 'so much as sticking a knife into the Heath'; but turf-cutting is carried on surreptitiously on all the outskirts of the Heath, for there used to be a sort of feeling, I was told, among some real Londoners that Hampstead Heath yielded the best turf of any place. All the 'commons' and 'greens', Paddington, Camberwell, Kennington, Clapham, Putney, &c. are also forbidden ground to the turf-cutter. 'O, as to the parks and Primrose Hill itself – round about it's another thing – nobody,' it was answered to my inquiry, 'ever thought of cutting their turf there. The people about, if they was only visitors, wouldn't stand it, and right too. I wouldn't, if I wasn't in the turf-cutting myself.'

The places where the turf is principally cut are the fields, or plots, in the suburbs, in which may be seen a half-illegible board, inviting the attention of the class of speculating builders to an 'eligible site' for villas. Some of these places are open, and have long been open, tithe road; others are protected by a few crazy rails, and the turf-cutters consider that outside the rails, or between them and the road, they have a *right* to cut turf, unless forbidden by the police. The fact is, that they cut it on sufferance; but the policeman never interferes, unless required to do so by the proprietor of the land or his agent. One gentleman, who has the control over a considerable quantity of land 'eligible' for building, is very inimical to the pursuits of the turf-cutters, who, of course, return his hostility. One man told me that he was re-quired, late on a Saturday night, some weeks ago, to supply six dozen of turfs to a very respectable shopkeeper, by ten or eleven on the Sunday morning. The shopkeeper had an aristocratic connection, and durst not disappoint his customers in their demands for fresh turf on the Sunday, so that the cutter must supply it. In doing so, he encountered Mr – (the gentleman in question), who was exceedingly angry with him: 'You damned poaching thief!' said the gentleman, 'if this is the way you pass your Sunday, I'll give you in charge.' One turf-cutter, I was informed, had, within these eight years, paid three pounds fifteen shillings in fines for trespassing, besides losing his barrow, &c., on every conviction.

'But he's a most outdacious fellor,' I was told by one of his mates, 'and won't mind spoiling anybody's ground to save hisself a bit of trouble. There's too many that way, which gives us a bad name.' Some of the managers of the land to be built upon give the turf-cutters free leave to labour in their vocation; others sell the sods for garden-plots, or use them to set out the gardens to any small houses they may be connected with, and with them the turf-cutters have no chance of turning a sod or a penny.

I accompanied a turf-cutter, to observe the manner of his work. We went to the neighbourhood of Highgate, which we reached a little before nine in the morning. There was nothing very remarkable to be observed, but the scene was not without its interest. Although it was nearly the middle of January, the grass was very green and the weather very mild. There happened to be no one on the ground but my companion and myself, and in some parts of our progress nothing was visible but green fields with their fringe of dark-coloured leafless trees; while in other parts, which were somewhat more elevated, glimpses of the crowded roof of an omnibus, or of a line of fleecy white smoke, showing the existence of a railway, testified to the neighbourhood of a city; but no sound was heard except, now and then, a distant railway whistle. The turf-cutter, after looking carefully about him – the result of habit, for I was told afterwards, by the policeman, that there was no trespass – set rapidly to work. His apparatus was a sharp-pointed table-knife of the ordinary size, which he inserted in the ground, and made it rapidly describe a half-circle; he then as rapidly ran his implement in the opposite half-circle, flung up the sod, and, after slapping it with his knife, cut off the lower part so as to leave it flat – working precisely as does a butcher cutting out a joint or a chop, and reducing the fat. Small holes are thus left in the ground of such shape and size as if deep saucers whereto be fitted into them – and in the event of a thunder-shower in droughty weather, they become filled with water, and have caused a puzzlement, I am told, to persons taking their quiet walk when the storm had ceased, to comprehend why the rain should be found to gather in little circular pools in some parts, and not in others.

The man I accompanied cut and shaped six of these turfs in about a minute, but he worked without intermission, and rather to show me with what rapidity and precision he could cut, than troubling himself to select what was saleable. After that we diverged in the direction of Hampstead; and in a spot not far from a temporary church, found three turf-cutters at work, – but they worked asunder, and without communication one with another. The turfs, as soon as they are cut and shaped, are thrown into a circular basket, and when the basket is full it is emptied on to the barrow (a costermonger's barrow), which is generally left untended at the nearest point: 'We can trust one another, as far as I know,' said one turf-man to me, 'and nobody else would find it worth while to steal turfs'. The largest number of men that my most intelligent informant had ever seen at work-in one locality was fourteen, and that was in afield just about to be built over, and 'where they had leave'. Among the turf-purveyors there is no understanding as to where they are to 'cut'. Wet weather does not interfere with turf procuring; it merely adds to the weight, and consequently to the toil of drawing the barrow. Snow is rather an advantage to the street-seller, as purchasers are apt to fancy that if the storm continues, turfs will not be obtainable, and so they buy more freely. The turf-man clears the snow from the ground in any known locality – the cold pinching his ungloved hands – and cuts out the turf, 'as green', I was told, 'as an April sod'. The weather most dreaded is that when hoar frost lies long and heavy on the ground, for the turf cut with the rime upon it soon turns black, and is unsaleable. Foggy dark weather is also prejudicial, 'for then', one man said, 'the days clips it uncommon short, and people won't buy by candlelight, no more will the shops. Birds has gone to sleep then, and them that's fondest on them says,

"We can get fresher turf tomorrow."' The gatherers cannot work by moonlight; 'for the clover leaves then shuts up,' I was told by one who said he was a bit of a botanist, 'like the lid of a box, and you can't tell them'.[16]

Nightmen at work

Nightwork is carried on – and has been so carried on, within the memory of the oldest men in the trade, who had never heard their predecessors speak of any other system – after this method:–
A gang of four men (exclusive of those who have the care of the horses, and who drive the night-carts to and from the scenes of the men's labours at the cesspools) are set to work. The labour of the gang is divided, though not with any individual or especial strictness, as follows:–

1. The holeman, who goes into the cesspool and fills the tub.
2. The ropeman, who raises the tub when filled.
3. The tubmen (of whom there are two), who carry away the tub when raised, and empty it into the cart.

The mode of work may be thus briefly described:—Within a foot, or even less sometimes, though often as much as three feet, below the surface of the ground (when the cesspool is away from the house) is what is called the "main hole". This is the opening of the cesspool, and is covered with flag stones, removable, wholly or partially, by means of the pickaxe. If the cesspool be immediately under the privy, the flooring, &c., is displaced. Should the soil be near enough to the surface, the tub is dipped into it, drawn out, the filth scraped from its exterior with a shovel, or swept off with a besom, or washed off by water flung against it with sufficient force. This done, the tubmen insert the pole through the handles of the tub, and bear it on their shoulders to the cart. The mode of carriage and the form of the tub have been already shown in an illustration, which I was assured by a nightman who had seen it in a shop window (for he could not read), was "as nat'ral as life, tub and all".

Thus far, the ropeman and the holeman generally aid in filling the tub, but as the soil becomes lower, the vessel is let down and drawn up full by the ropeman. When the soil becomes lower still, a ladder is usually planted inside the cesspool; the 'holeman', who is generally the strongest person in the gang, descends, shovels the tub full, having stirred up the refuse to loosen it, and the contents, being drawn up by the ropeman, are carried away as before described.

The labour is sometimes severe. The tub when filled, though it is never quite filled, weighs rarely less than eight stone, and sometimes more; 'but that, you see, sir,' a nightman said to me, 'depends on the nature of the sile'.

Beer, and bread and cheese, are given to the nightmen, and frequently gin, while at their work; but as the bestowal of the spirit is voluntary, some householders from motives of economy, or from being real or pretended members or admirers of the total-abstinence principles, refuse to give any strong liquor, and in that case – if such a determination to withhold the drink be known beforehand – the employers sometimes supply the men with a glass or two; and the men, when 'nothing better can be done', club their own money, and send to some night-house, often at a distance, to purchase a small quantity on their own account. One master-nightman said, he thought his men worked best, indeed he was sure of it, 'with a drop to keep them up'; another thought it did them neither good nor harm, 'in a moderate way of taking it'. Both these informants were themselves temperate men, one rarely tasting spirits. It is commonly enough said, that if the nightmen have no 'allowance', they will work

neither as quickly nor as carefully as if accorded the customary gin 'perquisite'. One man, certainly a very strong active person, whose services where quickness in the work was indispensable might be valuable (and he had work as a rubbish-carter also), told me that he for one would not work for any man at night-work if there was not a fair allowance of drink, 'to keep up his strength', and he knew others of the same mind. On my asking him what he considered a 'fair' allowance, he told me that at least a bottle of gin among the gang of four was 'looked for, and mostly had, over a gentleman's cesspool. And little enough, too,' the man said, 'among four of us; what it holds if it's public-house gin is uncertain: for you must know, sir, that some bottles has great "kicks" at their bottoms. But I should say that there's been a bottle of gin drunk at the clearing of every two, ay, and more than every two, out of three cesspools emptied in London; and now that I come to think on it, I should say that's been the case with three out of every four.'

Some master-nightmen, and more especially the sweeper-nightmen, work at the cesspools themselves, although many of them are men 'well to do in the world'. One master I met with, who had the reputation of being 'warm', spoke of his own manual labour in shovelling filth in the same self-complacent tone that we may imagine might be used by a grocer, worth his 'plum', who quietly intimates that he will serve a washerwoman with her half ounce of tea, and weigh it for her himself, as politely as he would serve a duchess; for he wasn't above his business: neither was the nightman.

On one occasion I went to see a gang of nightmen at work. Large horn lanterns (for the night was dark, though at intervals the stars shone brilliantly) were placed at the edges of the cess-pool. Two poles also were temporarily fixed in the ground, to which lanterns were hung, but this is not always the case. The work went rapidly on, with little noise and no confusion.

The scene was peculiar enough. The artificial light, shining into the dark filthy-looking cavern or cesspool, threw the adjacent houses into a deep shade. All around was perfectly still, and there was not an incident to interrupt the labour, except that at one time the window of a neighbouring house was thrown up, a night-capped head was protruded, and then down was banged the sash with an impatient curse. It appeared as if a gentleman's slumbers had been disturbed, though the nightmen laughed and declared it was a lady's voice! The smell, although the air was frosty, was for some little time, perhaps ten minutes, literally sickening; after that period the chief sensation experienced was a slight headache; the unpleasantness of the odour still continuing, though without any sickening effect. The nightmen, however, pronounced the stench 'nothing at all'; and one even declared it was refreshing!

The cesspool in this case was so situated that the cart or rather wagon could be placed about three yards from its edge; sometimes, however, the soil has to be carried through a garden and through the house, to the excessive annoyance of the inmates. The nightmen whom I saw evidently enjoyed a bottle of gin, which had been provided for them by the master of the house, as well as some bread and cheese, and two pots of beer. When the wagon was full, two horses were brought from a stable on the premises (an arrangement which can only be occasionally carried out) and yoked to the vehicle, which was at once driven away; a smaller cart and one horse being used to carry off the residue.[17]

Rhubarb and spice

Mayhew spoke to an Arab from Morocco who sold rhubarb and spice. The man had left his homeland when he was in his teens, but still spoke with a strong accent many years later.

I buy my rhubarb and my spice of de large warehouse for de drugs; sometime I buy it of my countreemen. We all of us know de good spice from de bad. You look! I will show you how to tell de good nutmeg from de bad. Here is some in de shell: you see, I put de strong pin in one and de oil run out; dat is because dey has not been put in de spirit to take away de oil for to make de extract. Now, in de bad nutmeg all de oil been took out by de spirit, and den dere is no flavour, like dose you buy in de sheep sops [cheap shops]. I sell de Rhubarb, East Indy and Turkey, de Cloves, Cinnamons, Mace, Cayenne Pepper, White Pepper – a little of all sorts when I get de money to buy it wid. I take my solemn oat I never sheat in scales nor weight; because de law is, 'take weight and give weight', dat is judge and justice. Dere is no luck in de sort [short] weight – no luck at all. Never in my life I put no tings wid my goods. I tell you de troot, I grind my white pepper wid my own hands, but I buy me ginger ground, and *dat* is mixed I know. I tink it is pea flour dey put wid it, dere is no smell in dat, but it is de same colour – two ounces of ginger will give de smell to one pound of pea flour. De publichouses *will* have de sheap ginger and dat I buy.[18]

'What a man larns in his fingers he never forgets'

I made rope traces for the artillery; there's a good deal of leather-work about the traces, and stitching them, you see, puts me up to the making of dogs' collars. I was always handy with my fingers, and can make shoes or anythink. I can work now as well as ever I could in my life, only my eyes isn't so good. Ain't it curious now, sir, that wot a man larns in his fingers he never forgets?[19]

Food sold through the seasons

The general dealer 'works' everything through the season. He generally begins the year with sprats or plaice: then he deals in soles until the month of May. After this he takes to mackerel, haddocks, or red herrings. Next he trades in strawberries or raspberries. From these he will turn to green and ripe gooseberries; thence he will go to cherries; from cherries he will change to red or white currants; from them to plums or greengages, and from them again to apples and pears, and damsons. After these he mostly 'works' a few vegetables, and continues with them until the fish season begins again. Some general dealers occasionally trade in sweetmeats, but this is not usual, and is looked down upon by the 'trade'.[20]

Patter for selling miscellaneous articles

These men have several articles which they sell singly, such as tea-trays, copper kettles, fire-irons, guns, whips, to all of which they have some preamble; but their most attractive lot is a heap of miscellaneous articles:

I have here a pair of scissors; I only want half-a-crown for them. What! you won't give a shilling? Well, I'll add something else. Here's a most useful article – a knife with eight blades, and there's not a blade among you all that's more highly polished. This knife's a case of instruments in addition to the blades; here's a corkscrew, a button-hook, a file, and a picker. For this capital knife and first-rate pair of scissors I ask one shilling. Well, well, you've no more conscience than a lawyer; here's something else – a pocket-book. This book no gentleman should be without; it contains a diary for every day in the week, an almanack, a ready-reckoner, a tablet for your own memorandums, pockets to keep your papers, and a splendid pencil with a silver top. No buyers! I'm astonished; but I'll add another article. Here's a pocket-comb. No young man with any sense of decency should be without a pocket-comb. What looks worse than to see a man's head in an uproar? Some of you look as if your hair hadn't seen a comb for years. Surely I shall get a customer now. What! no buyers – well I never! Here, I'll add half-a-dozen of the very best Britannia metal tea-spoons, and if you don't buy, you must be spoons yourselves. Why, you perfectly astonish me! I really believe if I was to offer all in the shop, myself included, I should not draw a shilling out of you. Well, I'll try again. Here, I'll add a dozen of black-lead pencils. Now, then, look at these articles [he spreads them out, holding them between his fingers to the best advantage] – here's a pair of first rate scissors, that will almost cut of themselves, – this valuable knife, which comprises within itself almost a chest of tools, – a splendid pocketbook, which must add to the respectability and consequence of any man who wears it, – a pocket comb which possesses the peculiar property of making the hair curl, and dyeing it any colour you wish, – a half-dozen spoons, nothing inferior to silver, and that do not require half the usual quantity of sugar to sweeten your tea, – and a dozen beautiful pencils, at least worth the money I ask for the whole lot. Now, a reasonable price for these articles would be at least ten shillings and sixpence; I'll sell them for one shilling, I ask no more, I'll take no less. Sold again![21]

Clarinet player makes own teeth

One of the blind makes his own teeth, he told me; his front ones have all been replaced by one long bit of bone which he has fastened to the stumps of his two eye teeth: he makes them out of any old bit of bone he can pick up. He files them and drills a hole through them to fasten them into his head, and eats his food with them. He is obliged to have teeth because he plays the clarinet in the street. 'Music,' he said, 'is our only enjoyment, we all like to listen to it and learn it.' It affects them greatly, they tell me, and if a lively tune is played, they can hardly help dancing. 'Many a tune I've danced to so that I could hardly walk the next day,' said one.[22]

Skilful pickpocket demonstrates

This lad picked my pocket at my request, and so dexterously did he do his 'work', that though I was alive to what he was trying to do, it was impossible for me to detect the least movement of my coat. To see him pick the pockets, as he did, of some of the gentlemen who were present on the occasion, was a curious sight. He crept behind much like a cat with his claws out, and while in the act held his breath with suspense; but immediately the handkerchief was safe in his hand, the change in the expression of his countenance was most marked. He then seemed almost to be convulsed with delight at the success of his perilous adventure, and, turning his back, held up the handkerchief to discover the value of his prize, with intense glee evident in every feature.[23]

Poetry skills

'Writing poetry is no comfort to me in my sickness. It might if I could write just what I please. The printers like hanging subjects best, and I don't. But when any of them sends to order a copy of verses for a "Sorrowful Lamentation" of course I must supply them. I don't think much of what I've done that way. If I'd my own fancy, I'd keep writing acrostics, such as one I wrote on our rector.' 'God bless him,' interrupted the wife, 'he's a good man.' 'That he is,' said the poet, 'but he's never seen what I wrote about him, and perhaps never will.' He then desired his wife to reach him his big Bible, and out of it he handed me a piece of paper, with the following lines written on it, in a small neat hand enough:

C elestial blessings hover round his head,
H undreds of poor, by his kindness were fed,
A nd precepts taught which he himself obeyed.
M an, erring man, brought to the fold of God,
P reaching pardon through a Saviour's blood.
N o lukewarm priest, but firm to Heaven's cause;
E xamples showed how much he loved its laws.
Y outh and age, he to their wants attends,
S teward of Christ – the poor man's sterling friend.[24]

'Love and sweethearting' with servant girls

I sell to women of all sorts. Smart-dressing servant-maids, perhaps, are my best customers, especially if they live a good way from any grand ticketing shop. I sold one of my umbrellas to one of them just before you spoke to me. She was standing at the door, and I saw her give half a glance at the umbrellas, and so I offered them. She first agreed to buy a very nice one at three shillings and threepence (which should have been four shillings), but I persuaded her to take one at three and ninepence (which should have been four and sixpence.). 'Look here, ma'am,' said I, 'this umbrella is much bigger you see, and will carry double, so when you're coming from church of a wet Sunday evening, a friend can have share of it, and very grateful he'll be, as he's sure to have his best hat on. There's been many a question put under an umbrella that way that's made a young lady blush, and take good care of her umbrella when she was married, and had a house of her own. I look sharp after the young and pretty ladies, Miss, and shall as long as I'm a bachelor.' 'O,' says she, 'such ridiculous nonsense. But I'll have the bigger umbrella, because it's often so windy about here, and then one must have a good cover if it rains as well.' That's my way, sir. I don't mind telling that, because they do the same in the shops. I've heard them, but they can't put love and sweethearting so cleverly in a crowded shop as we can in a quiet house. It's that I go for, love and sweet-hearting; and I always speak to any smart servant as if I thought she was the mistress, or as if I wasn't sure whether she was the mistress or the lady's-maid; three times out of four she's house-maid or maid of all work. I call her 'ma'am', and 'young lady', and sometimes 'miss'.[25]

Chapter Four: Scams and Frauds

There is an uncensorious quality about Mayhew's writing when he deals with the seamier side of London life. Many poor working people were driven to cheat their customers as a result of the very human reaction to people who were better off than they were and could, perhaps, afford to be defrauded. As one cheating tradesman says to Mayhew, 'People just brings it on themselves, by wanting things for next to nothing; so it's all right; it's people's own faults.' Another says 'I delight to do it with stingy aristocrats.' The practices Mayhew heard about range from the almost innocuous to the downright criminal, and, as usual with his writing, he was more interested in reporting accurately what went on than spending time condemning the perpetrators.

Boiling oranges

I shall now treat of the tricks of trade practised by the London costermongers. Of these the costers speak with as little reserve and as little shame as a fine gentleman of his peccadilloes. 'I've boiled lots of oranges,' chuckled one man, 'and sold them to Irish hawkers, as wasn't wide awake, for stunning big 'uns. The boiling swells the oranges and so makes 'em look finer ones, but it spoils them, for it takes out the juice. People can't find that out though until it's too late. I boiled the oranges only a few minutes, and three or four dozen at a time.'[26]

Hucksters

The hucksters usually start on their rounds about nine. There are very few who take money; indeed they profess to take none at all. 'But that is all flam,' said my informant. 'If any one was to ask me the price of an article in an artful way like, I shouldn't give him a straightforward answer. To such parties we always say, "Have you got any old clothes?"'

The hucksters *do* take money when they can get it, and they adopt the principle of exchanging their goods for old clothes merely as a means of evading the licence. Still they are compelled to do a great deal in the old clothes line. When they take money they usually reckon to get fourpence in the shilling, but at least three-fourths of their transactions consist of exchanges for old clothes. 'A good tea-service we generally give,' said my informant,

for a left-off suit of clothes, hat, and boots – they must all be in a decent condition to be worth that. We give a sugar-basin for an old coat, and a rummer for a pair of old Wellington boots. For a glass milk-jug I should expect a waistcoat and trousers, and they must be tidy ones too. But there's nothing so saleable as a pair of old boots to us. There is always a market for old boots, when there is not for old clothes. You can any day get a dinner out of old Wellingtons; but as for coats and waistcoats – there's a fashion about them, and what pleases one don't another. I can sell a pair of old boots going along the streets if I carry them in my hand. The snobs will run after us to get them – the backs are so valuable. Old beaver hats and waistcoats are worth little or nothing. Old silk hats, however, there's a tidy market for. They are bought for the shops, and are made up into new hats for the country. The shape is what is principally wanted. We won't give a farden for the polka hats with the low crowns. If we can double an old hat up and put it in our pockets, it's more valuable to us than a stiff one. We know that the shape must be good to stand that. As soon as a hatter touches a hat he knows by the touch or the stiffness of it whether it's been 'through' the fire or not; and if so, they'll give it you back in a minute. There is one man who stands in Devonshire-street, Bishopsgate-street, waiting to buy the hats of us as we go into the market, and who purchases at least thirty dozen of us a week. There will be three or four there besides him looking out for us as we return from our rounds, and they'll either outbid one another, according as the demand is, or they'll all hold together to give one price. The same will be done by other parties wanting the old umbrellas that we bring back with us. These are valuable principally for the whalebone. Cane ribbed ones are worth only from a penny to tuppence, and that's merely the value of the stick and the supporters. Iron skewers are made principally out of the old supporters of umbrellas.

The china and crockery bought by the hucksters at the warehouses are always second-rate articles. They are most of them a little damaged, and the glass won't stand hot water. Every huckster, when he starts, has a bag, and most of them two – the one for the inferior, and the other for the better kind of old clothes he buys. 'We purchase gentlemen's leftoff wearing apparel. This is mostly sold to us by women. They are either the wives of tradesmen or mechanics who sell them to us, or else it is the servant of a lodging-house, who has had the things given to her, and with her we can deal much easier than the others. She's come to 'em light, and of course she parts with 'em light,' said the man, 'and she'll take a pair of sugar basins worth about 6d., you know, for a thing that'll fetch two or three shillings sometimes.'[27]

'Slangs' – false weights

There's plenty of costers wouldn't use slangs at all, if people would give a fair price; but you see the boys *will* try it on for their bunts, and how is a man to sell fine cherries at fourpence a pound that cost him threepence ha'penny, when there's a kid alongside of him a selling his 'tol' at twopence a pound, and singing it out as bold as brass? So the men slangs it, and cries 'twopence a pound', and gives half-pound, as the boy does; which brings it to the same thing...

The slang quart is a pint and a half. It is made precisely like the proper quart; and the maker, I was told, 'knows well enough what it's for, as it's charged, new, sixpence more than a true quart measure; but it's nothing to him, as he says, what it's for, so long as he gets his price'. The slang quart is let out at twopence a day, a penny extra being charged 'for the risk'. The slang pint holds in some cases three-fourths of the just quantity, having a very thick bottom; others hold only half a pint, having a false bottom half-way up. These are used chiefly in measuring nuts, of which the proper quantity is hardly ever given to the purchaser. 'But, then,' it was often said, or implied to me, the 'price is all the lower, and people just brings it on themselves, by wanting things for next to nothing; so it's all right; it's people's own faults.'

The scales used are almost all true, but the weights are often beaten out flat to look large, and are 4, 5, 6, or even 7 oz. deficient in a pound, and in the same relative proportion with other weights. The charge is twopence, threepence, and fourpence a day for a pair of scales and a set of slang weights.

The wooden measures – such as pecks, half pecks, and quarter pecks – are not let out slang, but the bottoms are taken out by the costers, and put in again half an inch or so higher up.

'I call this,' said a humorous dealer to me, 'slopwork, or the cutting-system.'[28]

Cheating with true measures

One candid costermonger expressed his perfect contempt of slangs, as fit only for bunglers, as *he* could always 'work slang' with a true measure. 'Why, I can cheat any man,' he said. 'I can manage to measure mussels so as you'd think you got a lot over, but there's a lot under measure, for I holds them up with my fingers and keep crying, "Mussels! full measure, live mussels!" I can do the same with peas. I delight to do it with stingy aristocrats. We don't work slang in the City. People know what they're a buying on there. There's plenty of us would pay for an inspector of weights; I would. We might do fair without an inspector, and make as much if we only agreed one with another.'[29]

Reusing dead eels

The more honest costermongers will throw away fish when it is unfit for consumption; less scrupulous dealers, however, only throw away what is utterly unsaleable; but none of them fling away the dead eels, though their prejudice against such dead fish prevents their indulging in eel-pies. The dead eels are mixed with the living, often in the proportion of 20 lb. dead to 5 lb. alive, equal quantities of each being accounted very fair dealing. 'And after all,' said a street fish dealer to me, 'I don't know why dead eels should be objected to; the aristocrats don't object to them. Nearly all fish is dead before it's cooked, and why not eels? Why not eat them when they're sweet, if they're ever so dead, just as you eat fresh herrings? I believe it's only among the poor and among our chaps, that there's this prejudice. Eels die quickly if they're exposed to the sun.' Herrings are made to look fresh and bright by candle-light, by the lights being so disposed 'as to give them', I was told, 'a good reflection. Why I can make them look splendid; quite a picture. I can do the same with mackerel, but not so prime as herrings.'[30]

Smoking fish that are off

I've bought fish of costers that was over on a Saturday night, to make Scotch haddies of them. I've tried experience [experiments] too. Ivy, burnt under them, gave them, I thought, a nice sort of flavour, rather peppery, for I used always to taste them; but I hate living on fish. Ivy with brown berries on it, as it has about this time o' year, I liked best. Holly wasn't no good. A blackcurrant bush was, but it's too dear; and indeed it couldn't be had. I mostly spread wetted firewood, as green as could be got, or damp sticks of any kind, over shavings, and kept feeding the fire. Sometimes I burnt sawdust. Somehow, the dry fish trade fell off. People does get so prying and so knowing, there's no doing nothing now for no time, so I dropped the dry fish trade. There's few up to smoking them proper; they smoke 'em black, as if they was hung up in a chimbley. There's Scotch haddies that never knew anything about Scotland, for I've made lots of them myself by Tower-street, just a jump or two from the Lambeth station-house. I used to make them on Sundays. I was a wet fish-seller then, and when I couldn't get through my haddocks or my whitings of a Saturday night, I wasn't a-going to give them away to folks that wouldn't take the trouble to lift me out of a gutter if I fell there, so I preserved them. I've made haddies of whitings, and good ones too, and Joe made them of codlings besides. I had a bit of a back-yard to two rooms, one over the other, that I had then, and on a Sunday I set some wet wood a fire, and put it under a great tub. My children used to gut and wash the fish, and I hung them on hooks all round the sides of the tub, and made a bit of a chimney in a corner of the top of the tub, and that way I gave them a jolly good smoking. My wife had a dry fish-stall and sold them, and used to sing out 'Real Scotch haddies', and tell people how they was from Aberdeen; I've often been fit to laugh, she did it so clever. I had a way of giving them a yellow colour like the real Scotch, but that's a secret. After they was well smoked they was hung up to dry all round the rooms we lived in, and we often had stunning fires that answered as well to boil crabs and lobsters when they was cheap enough for the streets.[31]

Blowing up fish

Very cheap fish-sellers lose their customers, through the Billingsgate bummarees, for they have pipes, and blow up the cod-fish, most of all, and puff up their bellies till they are twice the size, but when it comes to table, there's hardly to say any fish at all. The Billingsgate authorities would soon stop it, if they knew all I know. They won't allow any roguery, or any trick, if they only come to hear of it. These bummarees have caused many respectable people to avoid street-buying, and so fair traders like me are injured.[32]

Price cartel among Jews

I go to Billingsgate to buy my fish, and am very well known to Mr — and Mr — [mentioning the names of some well-known salesmen]. The Jews are my ruin there now. When I go to Billingsgate, Mr — will say, or rather, I will say to him, 'How much for this pad of soles?' He will answer, 'Fourteen shillings.' 'Fourteen shillings!' I say, 'I'll give you seven shillings, – that's the proper amount.' Then the Jew boys – none of them twenty that are there – ranged about will begin; and one says, when I bid seven shillings, 'I'll give eight shillings'; 'Nine,' says another, close on my left; 'Ten,' shouts another, on my right, and so they go offering on; at last Mr — says to one of them, as grave as a judge, 'Yours, sir, at thirteen shillings,' but it's all gammon. The thirteen shilling buyer isn't a buyer at all, and isn't required to pay a farthing, and never touches the goods. It's all done to keep up the price to poor fishmen, and so to poor buyers that are our customers in the streets.[33]

Faked murders sheets

The murders are bought by men, women, and children. Many of the tradespeople bought a great many of the affair of the Mannings. I went down to Deptford with mine, and did uncommonly well. I sold all off. Gentlefolks won't have anything to do with murders sold in the street; they've got other ways of seeing all about it. We lay on the horrors, and picture them in the highest colours we can. We don't care what's in the 'papers' in our hands. All we want to do is to sell 'em; and the more horrible we makes the affairs, the more sale we have. We do very well with 'love letters'. They are 'cocks'; that is, they are all fictitious. We give it out that they are from a tradesman in the neighbourhood, not a hundred yards from where we are a-standing. Sometimes we say it's a well-known sporting butcher; sometimes it's a highly respectable publican – just as it will suit the tastes of the neighbourhood. I got my living round Cornwall for one twelvemonth with nothing else than a love letter. It was headed, 'A curious and laughable love-letter and puzzle, sent by a sporting gentleman to Miss H–s–m, in *this* neighbourhood'; that suits any place that I may chance to be in; but I always patter the name of the street or village where I may be. This letter, I say, is so worded, that had it fallen into the hands of her mamma or papa, they could not have told what it meant; but the young lady, having so much wit, found out its true meaning, and sent him an answer in the same manner. You have here, we say, the number of the house, the name of the place where she lives (there is nothing of the kind, of course), and the initials of all the parties concerned. We dare not give the real names in full, we tell them; indeed, we do all we can to get up the people's curiosity...

I did very well with the 'Burning of the House of Commons'. I happened by accident to put my pipe into my pocket amongst some of my papers, and burnt them. Then, not knowing how to get rid of them, I got a few straws. I told the people that my burnt papers were parliamentary documents that had been rescued from the flames, and that, as I dare not sell them, I would let them have a straw for a penny, and give them one of the papers. By this trick I got rid of my stock twice as fast, and got double the price that I should have done. The papers had nothing at all to do with the House of Commons. Some was 'Death and the Lady', and 'Death and the Gentleman', and others were the 'Political Catechism', and '365 lies, Scotch, English, and Irish', and each lie as big round as St Paul's.[34]

The 'selling cotton' con

An inmate of one of the low lodging-houses has supplied me with the following statement:

Within my recollection, the great branch of trade among these worthies, was the sale of sewing cotton, either in skeins or on reels. In the former case, the article cost the 'lurkers' about eightpence per pound; one pound would produce thirty skeins, which, sold at one penny each, or two for three halfpence, produced a heavy profit. The lurkers could mostly dispose of three pounds per day; the article was, of course, damaged, rotten, and worthless.

The mode of sale consisted in the 'lurkers' calling at the several houses in a particular district, and representing themselves as Manchester cotton spinners out of employ. Long tales, of course, were told of the distresses of the operatives, and of the oppression of their employers; these tales had for the most part been taught them at the padding-ken, by some old and experienced dodger of 'the school;' and if the spokesman could patter well, a much larger sum was frequently obtained in direct alms than was reaped by the sale.

Cotton on reels was – except to the purchaser – a still better speculation; the reels were large, handsomely mounted, and displayed in bold relief such inscriptions as the following:

PIKE'S PATENT COTTON
120 Yards.

The reader, however, must divide the 120 yards here mentioned by twelve, and then he will arrive at something like the true secret as to the quantity; for the surface only was covered by the thread.

The 'cotton Lurk' is now 'cooper'd' (worn out); a more common dodge – and, of course, only an excuse for begging – is to envelope a packet of 'warranted' needles, or a few inches of 'real Honiton lace' in an envelope, with a few lines to the 'Lady of the House', or a printed bill, setting forth the misery of the manufacturers, and the intention of the parties leaving the 'fakement' to presume to call for an answer in a few hours. I subjoin a copy of one of these documents.

THE LACE-MAKERS' APPEAL.

It is with extreme regret we thus presume to trespass on your time and attention, we are Lace-Makers by trade, and owing to the extensive improvements in Machinery, it has made hand labour completely useless.

So that it has thrown hundreds of honest and industrious men out of employment, your petitioners are among the number. Fifteen men with their families have left their homes with the intention of emigrating to South Australia, and the only means we have of supporting ourselves till we can get away, is by the sale of some Frame Thread and Traced Lace Collars of our own manufacture, at the following low prices – Fashionable Frame Lace Collars threepence each, warranted to wash and wear well; Frame Thread Collars sixpence each, Traced Lace Collars one shilling each, the best that can be made, and we trust we shall meet with that encouragement from the Friends of Industry which our necessities require.

The party calling for this, will have an assortment of the Newest Patterns of Frame Thread Lace and Edgings for your inspection, and the smallest purchase will be thankfully received and gratefully remembered by G. DAVIS, Lace Makers.

We beg to state that a number of the families being destitute of clothing, the bearer is authorised to receive any articles of such in exchange for Lace, Edgings or Collars.

ALLEN, Printer, Long-row, Nottingham.

These are left by one of 'the school' at the houses of the gentry, a mark being placed on the door post of such as are 'bone' or 'gammy', in order to inform the rest of 'the school' where to call, and what houses to avoid. As the needles cost but a few pence per thousand, and the lace less than one halfpenny per yard – a few purchasers of the former at one shilling per packet (twenty-five needles), or of the latter at two shillings and sixpence per yard, is what these 'lurkers' term a 'fair day's work for a fair day's wages'.

Pat [Connor] 'does nothing on the blob', that is to say he does not follow people and speak to them on the streets. His 'dodge' – and it has been for years a successful one – is to go round to the public offices, dressed as before described, with the exception of being in his shirt sleeves (he has every day a *clean* shirt), and teaze the clerks till they purchase a pen-knife. He has been known to sell from fifteen to twenty knives in one day, at two shillings each, the first cost being about threepence-halfpenny. Of course he is often interrupted by porters and other officials, but he always carries in one hand a roll of wire, and a small hammer in the other, and having got the name of some gentleman up stairs, he pretends that he is going to mend Mr So-and-so's bell. This worthy, a short time ago, made free – in the Custom House – with a timepiece, belonging to one of the clerks, for which the 'Sheffield manufacturer' got twelve months in Newgate. I have not seen him since, and therefore imagine that he is now taking a provincial tour.[35]

Disguising badly made dolls

The legs and bodies is carefully wrapped in tissue paper, not exactly to preserve the lower part of the doll, for that isn't so very valuable, but in reality to conceal the legs and body, which is rather the reverse of symmetrical; for, to tell the truth, every doll looks as if it were labouring under an attack of the gout. There are, however, some very neat articles exported from Germany, especially the jointed dolls, but they are too dear for the street-hawker, and would not show to such advantage. There is also the plaster dolls, with the match legs. I wonder how they keep their stand, for they are very old-fashioned; but they sell, for you never see a chandler's shop window without seeing one of these sticking in it, and a falling down as if it was drunk.[36]

Doctoring damaged goods

My master [he said] was an Irishman, and told everybody he had been a manager of a linen factory in Belfast. I believe he was brought up to be a shoemaker, and was never in the north of Ireland. Anyhow, he was very shy of talking about Irish factories to Irish gentlemen. I heard one say to him, 'Don't tell me, you have the Cork brogue.' I know he'd got some know-ledge of linen weaving at Dundee, and could talk about it very clever; indeed he was a clever fellow. Sometimes, to hear him talk, you'd think he was quite a religious man, and at others that he was a big blackguard. It wasn't drink that made the difference, for he was no drinker. It's a great thing on a round to get a man or woman into a cheerful talk, and put in a joke or two; and that he could do, to rights ... He was a buyer of damaged goods, and we used to 'doctor' them. In some there was perhaps damages by two or three threads being out all the way, so the manufacturers wouldn't send them to their regular customers. My master pretended it was a secret where he got them, but, lord, I knew; it was at a swag-shop. We used to cut up these in twelves [twelve yards], sometimes less if they was very bad, and take a Congreve, and just scorch them here and there, where the flaws was worst, and plaster over other flaws with a little flour and dust, to look like a stain from street water from the fire-engine. Then they were from the stock of Mr Anybody, the great draper, that had his premises burnt down – in Manchester or Glasgow, or London – if there'd been a good fire at a draper's – or anywhere; we wasn't particular. They was fine or strong shirtings, he'd say – and so they was, the sound parts of them – and he'd sell as cheap as common calico. I've heard him say, 'Why, marm, sure marm, with your eyes and scissors and needle, them burns – ah! fire's a dreadful judgment on a man – isn't the least morsel of matter in life. The stains is cured in a wash-tub in no time. It's only *touched* by the fire, and you can humour it, I know, in cutting out as a shirt ought to be cut; it should be as carefully done as a coat.'

Then we had an Irish linen, an imitation, you know, a kind of 'Union', which we call double twist. It is made, I believe, in Manchester, and is a mixture of linen and cotton. Some of it's so good that it takes a judge to tell the difference between it and real Irish. He got some beautiful stuff at one time, and once sold to a fine-dressed young woman in Brompton, a dozen yards, at two shillings and sixpence a yard, and the dozen only cost him fourteen shillings…

Some of the fraternity [says my informant] do not always deal 'upon the square'; they profess to have just come from India or China, and to have invested all their capital in silks of a superior description manufactured in those countries, and to have got them on shore 'unbeknown to the Custom-house authorities'. This is told in confidence to the servant-man or woman who opens the door – 'Be so good as tell the lady as much,' says the hawker, 'for really I'm afraid to carry the goods much longer, and I have already sold enough to pay me well enough for my spec – go, there's a good girl, tell your missus I have splendid goods, and am willing almost to give them away, and if we makes a deal of it, why I don't mind giving you a handsome present for yourself.' This is a bait not to be resisted. Should the salesman succeed with the mistress, he carries out his promise to the maid by presenting her with a cap ribbon, or a cheap neckerchief.[37]

Lurks galore

On my way up from Chatham, I met at Gravesend with seven chaps out on 'the Spanish lurk' as they called it – that is, passing themselves off as wounded men of the Spanish Legion. Two *had been* out in Spain, and managed the business if questions were asked; the others were regular English beggars, who had never been out of the country. I joined them as a sergeant, as I had a sergeant's jacket given me at Chatham. On our way to London – 'the school' (as the lot is called) came all together – we picked up among us four and five pounds and a day – no matter where we went. 'The school' all slept in lodging-houses, and I at last began to feel comfortable in them. We spent our evenings in eating out-and-out suppers. Sometimes we had such things as sucking pigs, hams, mince pies – indeed we lived on the best. No nobleman could live better in them days. So much wine, too! I drank in such excess, my nose was as big as that there letter stamp; so that I got a sickening of it. We gave good victuals away that was given to us – it was a nuisance to carry them. It cost us from sixpence to a shilling a day to have our shoes cleaned by *poor* tramps, and for clean dickies. The clean dodge is always the best for begging upon.

At Woolwich we were all on the fuddle at the Dust Hole, and our two spokesmen were drunk; and I went to beg of Major – whose brother was then in Spain – he himself had been out previously. Meeting the major at his own house, I said, 'I was a sergeant in the 3rd Westminster Grenadiers, you know, and served under your brother.'

'Oh! yes, that's my brother's regiment,' says he. 'Where was you, then, on the 16th of October?'

'Why, sir, I was at the taking of the city of Irun,' says I. (In fact, I was at that time with the costermonger in St Giles's, calling cabbages, 'white heart cabbages, oh!')

Then said the major, 'What day was Ernani taken on?'

'Why,' said I (I was a little tipsy, and bothered at the question), 'that was the 16th of October, too.'

'Very well, my man,' says he, tapping his boots with a riding whip he held, 'I'll see what I can do for you'; and the words were no sooner out of his mouth than he stepped up to me and gave me a regular pasting. He horsewhipped me up and down stairs, and all along the passages; my flesh was like sausages. I managed at last, however, to open the door myself, and get away. After that 'the school' came to London. In a day we used to make from eight to ten pounds among us, by walking up Regent-street, Bond-street, Piccadilly, Pall Mall, Oxford-street, the parks – those places were the best beats. All the squares were good too. It was only like a walk out for air, and your twenty-five shillings a man for it. At night we used to go to plays, dressed like gentlemen. At first the beaks protected us, but we got found out, and the beaks grew rusty. The thing got so overdone, every beggar went out as a Spanish lurksman. Well, the beaks got up to the dodge, and all the Spanish lurksmen in their turns got to work the universal staircase, under the care of Lieutenant Tracy (Tothill-fields treadmill). The men that had really been out and got disabled were sent to that staircase at last, and I thought I would try a fresh lurk, so I went under the care and tuition of a sailor. He had been a sailor. I became a *turnpike sailor,* as it's called, and went out as one of the Shallow Brigade, wearing a Guernsey shirt and drawers, or tattered trowsers. There was a school of four. We only got a tidy living – sixteen shillings or a pound a day among us. We used to call every one that came along – coalheavers and all – seafighting captains. 'Now, my noble sea-fighting captain,' we used to say, 'fire an odd shot from your larboard locker to us, Nelson's bull-dogs.' But mind we never tried that dodge on at Greenwich, for fear of the old geese, the Collegemen. The Shallow got so grannied [known] in London, that the supplies got queer, and I quitted the land navy. Shipwrecks got so common in the streets, you see, that people didn't care for them, and I dropped getting cast away.

I then took to *screeving* (writing on the stones). I got my head shaved, and a cloth tied round my jaws, and wrote on the flags 'ILLNESS and WANT,' though I was never better in my life, and always had a good bellyfull before I started of a morning. I did very well at first: three or four shillings a day – sometimes more – till I got grannied. There is one man who draws Christ's heads with a crown of thorns, and mackerel, on the pavement, in coloured chalks (there are four or five others at the same business); this one, however, often makes a pound a day now in three hours; indeed, I have known him come home with twenty-one shillings, besides what he drank on the way. A gentleman who met him in Regent-street once gave him five pounds and a suit of clothes to do Christ's heads with a crown of thorns and mackerel on the walls. His son does Napoleon's heads best, but makes nothing like so much as the father. The father draws cats' heads and salmon as well – but the others are far the best spec. He will often give thirteen pence, and indeed fourteen pence, for a silver shilling, to get rid of the coppers. This man's pitch is Lloyd-square, not far from Sadler's Wells. I have seen him commence his pitch there at half-past eleven, to catch the people come from the theatre. He is very clever. In wet weather, and when I couldn't chalk, as I couldn't afford to lose time, I used to dress tidy and very clean for the 'respectable broken-down tradesman or reduced gentleman' caper. I wore a suit of black, generally, and a clean dickey, and sometimes old black kid gloves, and I used to stand with a paper before my face, as if ashamed: 'To a Humane Public'; 'I have seen better days'.

This is called standing pad with a fakement. It is a wet-weather dodge, and isn't so good as screeving, but I did middling, and can't bear being idle.

After this I mixed with the street patterers (men who make speeches in the streets) on the destitute mechanics' lurk. We went in a school of six at first, all in clean aprons, and spoke every man in his turn. It won't do unless you're clean. Each man wanted [lacked] a particular article of dress. One had no shirt – another no shoes – another no hat – and so on. No two wanted the same. We said:

Kind and benevolent Christians! It is with feelings of deep regret, and sorrow and shame, that us unfortunate tradesmen are compelled to appear before you this day, to ask charity from the hands of strangers. We are brought to it from want – I may say, actual starvation. ['We always had a good breakfast before we started, and some of us, sir, was full up to the brim of liquor.'] But what will not hunger and the cries of children compel men to do. ['We were all single men.'] When we left our solitary and humble homes this morning, our children were crying for food, but if a farthing would have saved their lives, we hadn't it to give them. I assure you, kind friends, me, my wife, and three children, would have been houseless wanderers all last night, but I sold the shirt from off my back as you may see (opening my jacket) to pay for a lodging. We are, kind friends, *English* mechanics. It is hard that you won't give your own countrymen a penny, when you give so much to *foreign* hurdy-gurdies and organ-grinders. Owing to the introduction of steam and machinery and foreign manufactures we have been brought to this degraded state. Fellow countrymen, there are at this moment 4,000 men like ourselves, able and willing to work, but can't get it, and forced to wander the streets. I hope and trust some humane Christian within the sound of my voice will stretch out a hand with a small trifle for us, be it ever so small, or a bit of dry bread or cold potato, or anything turned from your table, it would be of the greatest benefit to us and our poor children. ['Then we would whisper to one another, "I hope they won't bring out any scran – only coppers."'] We have none of us tasted food this blessed day. We have been told to go to our parishes, but that we cannot brook; to be torn from our wives and families is heart-rending to think of – may God save us all from the Bastille! [We always pattered hard at the overseers.]

The next of the school that spoke would change the story somehow, and try to make it more heartrending still. We did well at first, making about five shillings a day each, working four hours, two in the morning and two in the afternoon. We got a good deal of clothing too. The man who went without a shirt never went to a door to ask for one; he had to show himself in the middle of the road. The man that *did* go to the door would say, 'Do bestow a shirt on my poor shopmate, who hasn't had one for some days.' It's been said of me, when I had my shirt tied round my waist all the time out of sight. The man who goes without his shirt has his pick of those given; the rest are sold and shared. Whatever trade we represented we always had one or two really of the trade in the school. These were always to be met at the lodging-houses. They were out of work, and had to go to low lodging-houses to sleep. There they met with beggars who kiddied them on to the lurk. The lodging-houses is good schools for that sort of thing, and when a mechanic once gets out on the lurk he never cares to go to work again. I never knew one return. I have been out oft and oft with weavers with a loom, and have woven a piece of ribbon in a gentleman's parlour – that was when we was Coventry ribbon weavers. I have been a stocking weaver from Leicester, and a lacemaker too from Nottingham.

Distressed mechanics on their way to London get initiated into beggar's tricks in the low lodging-houses and the unions. This is the way, you see, sir. A school may be at work from the lodging-house where the mechanic goes to, and some of the school finds out what he is, and says, 'Come and work with us in a school: you'll do better than you can at your business, and you can answer any questions; we'll lurk on your trade.' I have been out with a woman and children. It's been said in the papers that children can be hired for that lurk at fourpence or sixpence a day – that's all fudge, all stuff, every bit of it – there's no children to be hired. There's many a labouring man out of work, who has a wife and three or more children, who is glad to let them go out with any patterer he knows. The woman is entitled to all the clothes and grub given, and her share of the tin – that's the way it's done; and she's treated to a drink after her day's work, into the bargain. I've been out on the *respectable family man* lurk. I was out with a woman and three kids the other day; her husband was on the pad in the country, as London was too hot to hold him. The kids draws, the younger the better, for if you vex them, and they're oldish, they'll blow you. Liverpool Joe's boy did so at Bury St Edmund's to a patterer that he was out with, and who spoke cross to him. The lad shouted out so as the people about might hear, 'Don't you jaw me, you're not my father; my father's at home playing cards.' They had to crack the pitch [discontinue] through that.

The respectable family dodge did pretty well. I've been on *the clean family* lurk too, with a woman and children. We dressed to give the notion that, however humble, at least we were clean in all our poverty. On this lurk we stand by the side of the pavement in silence, the wife in a perticler clean cap, and a milk-white apron. The kids have long clean pin-afores, white as the driven snow; they're only used in clean lurk, and taken off directly they come home. The husband and father is in a white flannel jacket, an apron worn and clean, and polished shoes. To succeed in this caper there must be no rags, but plenty of darns. A pack of pawn-tickets is carried in the waistcoat pocket. (One man that I know stuck them in his hat like a carman's.) That's to show that they've parted with their little all before they came to that. They are real pawn-tickets. I have known a man pay two and sixpence for the loan of a marriage certificate to go out on the clean lurk. If a question is asked, I say – 'We've parted with everything, and can get no employment; to be sure, we have had a loaf from the parish, but what's that among my family?' That takes the start out of the people, because they say, why not go to the parish? Some persons say, 'Oh, poor folks, they're brought to this, and how clean they are – a darn is better than a patch any time.' The clean lurk is a bare living now – it was good – lots of togs came in, and often the whole family were taken into a house and supplied with flannel enough to make under clothing for them all; all this was pledged soon afterwards, and the tickets shown to prove what was parted with, through want. Those are some of the leading lurks. There's others. 'Fits' are now bad, and 'para-lytics' are no better.

I'll tell you of another lurk: a woman I knows sends out her child with a quarter of an ounce of tea and half a quarter of sugar, and the child sits on a door step crying, and saying, if questioned, that she was sent out for tea and sugar, and a boy snatched the change from her, and threw the tea and sugar in the gutter. The mother is there, like a stranger, and says to the child: 'And was that your poor mother's last shilling, and daren't you go home, poor thing?'

Then there is a gathering – sometimes eighteen pence in a morning; but it's almost getting stale, that is.

I've done the shivering dodge too – gone out in the cold weather half naked. One man has practised it so much that he can't get off shivering now. Shaking Jemmy went on with his shivering so long that he couldn't help it at last. He shivered like a jelly – like a calf's foot with the ague – on the hottest day in summer. It's a good dodge in tidy inclement seasons. It's not so good a lurk, by two bob a day, as it once was. This is a single-handed job; for if one man shivers less than another he shows that it isn't so cold as the good shiverer makes it out – then it's no go … Why, from standing shaking – that is, being out nearly naked in the hardest frosts – I lost the use of my left side for nearly three years, and wasn't able to stir outside the door.[38]

Ring-dropping con

According to an informant, the ring-dropping 'lurk' is now carried on this way, for the old style is 'coopered'. 'A woman' he says, 'is made up so as to appear in the family-way – pretty far gone – and generally with a face as long as a boy's kite. Up she goes to any likely ken, where she knows there are women that are married or expect to get married, and commences begging. Then comes the tale of woe, if she can get them to listen.

'I'm in the family-way,' she says, 'as you can plainly see *young ladies*' (this she says to the *servants,* and that prides them you know). 'My husband has left me after serving me in this way. I don't know where he is, and am forced to solicit the ladies' charity.' Well, the servants will bring broken victuals and make a little collection among themselves for the 'unprotected female'; for which in return, with many thanks for their kindness, she offers her gold wedding-ring for sale, as she wants to get back to her suffering kids to give them something to eat, poor things, and they shall have the gold ring, she says, for half what it's worth; or if they won't buy it, will they lend 2s. or 3s. on it till she can redeem it, as she hasn't been in the habit of pledging! The girls are taken off their guard (she not being in the habit of pledging is a choker for them) by the woman's seeming simplicity, and there's a consultation. One says to the other 'Oh, you'll want it, Mary, for John'; and another, 'No, you'll want it first, Sally, for William.' But the woman has her eye on the one as says the least, as the likeliest of all to want it, and so she says to the John and William girls, 'Oh, you don't want it; but *here*' (touching the silent one), 'here's a *young lady* as does,' (that sweetens the servant girl up directly). She says, 'I don't want it, bless you (with a giggle), but I'll lend you a trifle, as you are in this state, and have a family, and are left like this by your husband – ain't he cruel, Sally (she adds to her fellow-servant)?' The money the ring-woman gets, sir, depends upon the servant's funds; if it is just after quarter-day, she generally gets a tidy tip – if not, four or five bob. I've known one woman get ten shillings and even twelve shillings this way. The ring is made out of brass gilt buttons, and stunning well: it's faked up to rights, and takes a good judge even at this day to detect it without a test...

The flyest cove among all us ring-sellers is little Ikey, the Jew. There were two used to work the game. They had a real gold ring, just like the ones they were selling, and they always used to pitch near a pawnbroker's shop. Ikey's pal would buy a ring for a penny, of the street-seller, and would then say, loud enough to be heard by the bystanders, 'There's a pawn shop – I'll go and ask them to take it in.' A crowd would follow him. He would enter the pawnbroker's – present a real gold ring – obtain a loan of five shillings, and would present the ticket to the bystanders, who would then buy very fast. When the pitch was over, Ikey's pal would take the ring out of pawn, and away the two would go to work near some other pawnbroker's. I have heard Ikey say they have pawned the ring thirty-five times in a day. I tried the same caper; but my pal cut with the gold ring the first day, and I've never had another go at that *fake* since… The second day I tried the ring dodge, I was a little more successful; indeed every day for some time exceeded the day before, for, as I improved in patter, my sales increased. My appearance, too, was improving. At one time I was a regular swell, sported white kid gloves, white choker, white waistcoat, black ribbon, and a quizzing glass. Some people used to chaff me, and cry out 'there's a swell'. I never was saving, always spent my money as fast as I got it. I might have saved a goodish bit, and I wish I had now.[39]

Chapter Five: A Street Photographer

One aspect of Mayhew's waywardness was his apparent lack of editing of his own material. To a certain extent this was a by-product of the fact that London Labour and the London Poor *was first published in weekly parts. As was the case with the writings of his friend Charles Dickens, if one don't know in detail what was coming next one's writings are likely to have a certain erratic quality about them, as expressed in the way in which one chapter can go in great detail into a tiny topic, while another spans a whole swathe of activities. In Mayhew's case, I suspect, the occasions on which he writes at length about a single topic or person are a result of his fascination with the subject and his inability to edit the material down to a manageable length. In Volume 3 of* London Labour and the London Poor, *for example, there is an account of a Punch and Judy man which runs to nearly 12,000 words.*

This chapter is devoted to a shorter but still substantial interview with a street photographer. In an era where the taking and viewing of photographs is a daily, if not hourly, occurrence, this account of the dawn of popular photography provides almost unbelievable revelations of the unfamiliarity most people had with their own appearance, and the ways in which that unfamiliarity could be turned to the photographer's advantage. It also shows the cumbersome nature of early photography and the learning curve that faced anyone taking it up as a profession.

I've been on and off at photographic portrait taking since its commencement – that is to say, since they were taken cheap – two years this summer. I lodged in a room in Lambeth, and I used to take them in the back-yard – a kind of garden; I used to take a blanket off the bed, and used to tack it on a clothes-horse, and my mate used to hold it, if the wind was high, whilst I took the portrait.

The reason why I took to photographing was, that I thought I should like it better than what I was at. I was out busking and drag-pitching with a banjo then. Busking is going into public-houses and playing, and singing, and dancing; and drag-pitching is going out in the day down the little courts – tidy places, little terraces, no thoroughfares, we call drags. I'm a very determined chap, and when I take an idea into my head I always do it somehow or other. I didn't know anything about photographs then, not a mite, but I saved up my money; sometimes a shilling; if I had a good day, one and sixpence; and my wife she went to work at day boot-binding, and at night dancing at a exhibition, or such-like (she's a tolerable good dancer – a penny exhibition or a parade dancer at fairs; that is, outside a show); sometimes she is Mademoiselle, or Madame,

or what it may be. I got a loan of £3 (and had to pay four pounds three shillings for it), and with what I'd saved, I managed to get together five guineas, and I went to Gilbert Flemming's, in Oxford-street, and bought a complete apparatus for taking pictures; 6½ by 4¾, for five guineas. Then I took it home, and opened the next day to take portraits for what we could get – a shilling and over. I never knew anything about taking portraits then, though they showed me when I bought the apparatus (but that was as good as nothing, for it takes months to learn). But I had cards ready printed to put in the window before I bought the apparatus. The very next day I had the camera, I had a customer before I had even tried it, so I tried it on him, and I gave him a black picture (for I didn't know how to make the portrait, and it was all black when I took the glass out), and told him that it would come out bright as it dried, and he went away quite delighted. I took the first Sunday after we had opened one pound, five shillings and sixpence and everybody was quite pleased with their spotted and black pictures, for we still told them they would come out as they dried. But the next week they brought them back to be changed, and I could do them better, and they had middling pictures – for I picked it up very quick.

I had one fellow for a half-guinea portrait, and he was from Woolwich, and I made him come three times, like a lamb, and he stood pipes and 'bacca, and it was a thundering bad one after all. He was delighted, and he swears now it's the best he ever had took, for it don't fade, but will stop black to the end of the world; though he remarks that I deceived him in one thing, for it don't come out bright.

You see, when first photography come up I had my eye on it, for I could see it would turn me in something some time. I went and worked as a regular labourer, carrying pails and so on, so as to try and learn something about chemistry; for

I always had a hankling after science. Me and Jim was out at Stratford, pitching with the banjo, and I saw some men coming out of a chemical works, and we went to 'nob' them (that's get some halfpence out of them). Jim was tambo beating, and we was both black, and they called us lazy beggars, and said we ought to work as they did. So we told them we couldn't get work, we had no characters. As we went home I and Jim got talking, and he says, 'What a fine thing if we could get into the berth, for you'd soon learn about them portraits if you get among the chemicals.' SoI agreed to go and try for the situation, and told him that if I got the berth I'd 'nanti panka his nabs snide'; that means, I wouldn't turn him up, or act nasty to him, but would share money the same as if we were pitching again. That slang is mummers' slang, used by strolling professionals.

I stopped there for near twelve months, on and off. I had ten shillings at first, but I got up to sixteen shillings; and if I'd stopped I've no doubt I should have been foreman of one of the departments, for I got at last to almost the management of the oxalic acid. They used to make sulphate of iron – ferri sulp is the word for it – and carbonate of iron, too, and I used to be like the red man of Agar then, all over red, and a'most thought of cutting that to go for a soldier, for I shouldn't have wanted a uniform. Then I got to charging the retorts to make carbonate of ammonia, and from that I went to oxalic acid.

At night me and Jim used to go out with the banjo and tamborine, and we could manage to make up our shares to from eighteen shillings to a guinea a-week each; that is, sharing my wages and all; for when we chum together we always panka each other bona (that is, share). We always made our ponta (that is, a pound) a-week, for we could average our duey bionk peroon a darkey', or two shillings each, in the night.

That's how I got an idea of chemicals, and when I went to photography many of the very things I used to manufacture was the very same as we used to take portraits, such as the hyposulphate of soda, and the nitrate of silver, and the sulphate of iron.

One of the reasons why I couldn't take portraits was, that when I bought my camera at Flemming's he took a portrait of me with it to show me how to use it, and as it was a dull afternoon he took ninety seconds to produce the picture. So, you see, when I went to work I thought I ought to let my pictures go the same time; and hang me if I didn't, whether the sun was shining or not. I let my plate stop ninety seconds, and of course they used to come out overdone and quite white, and as the evening grew darker they came better. When I got a good one I was surprised, and that picture went miles to be shown about. Then I formed an idea that I had made a miscalculation as to my time, and by referring to the sixpenny book of instructions I saw my mistake, and by the Sunday – that was five days after – I was very much improved, and by a month I could take a very tidy picture.

I was getting on so well I got some of my portraits, when they was good ones, put in a chandler's shop; and to be sure I got first-rate specimens. I used to go to the different shilling portrait galleries and have a likeness of myself or friends done, to exhibit in my own window. That's the way I got my samples to begin with, and I believe it's done all over London.

I kept at this all the winter, and all the time I suppose I earned thirty shillings a-week. When summer come again I took a place with a garden in the Old Kent-road, and there I done middling, but I lost the majority of my business by not opening on a Sunday, for it was a religious neighbourhood, and I could have earned my £5 a-week comfortable, for as it was I cleared my £2 regular. Then I had a regular tent built up out of clothes-horses. I stopped there till I had an offer of a good situation, and I accepted of it, at £2 a-week.

My new place was in Whitechapel, and we lowered the price from a shilling to sixpence. We did well there, that is the governor did, you know, for I've taken on the average from 60 to 100 a-day, varying in price from sixpence to half a-guinea, and the majority was shilling ones. The greatest quantity I ever took was 146 in one day, and 124 was taken away as they was done. The governor used to take £20 a-week, and of that £8 clear profit, after paying me £2 the men at the door twenty four shillings, a man and woman twenty-nine shillings, and rent £2. My governor had, to my knowledge, eleven other shops, and I don't know all of his establishments; I managed my concern for him, and he never come near us sometimes for a month.

I left on my own accord after four months, and I joined two others on equal shares, and opened a place of my own in Southwark. Unfortunately, I begun too late in the season, or I should have done well there; but at first we realised about £2 a-week each, and up to last week we have shared our twenty-five shillings a-head.

Sunday is the best day for shilling portraits; in fact, the majority is shilling ones, because then, you see, people have got their wages, and don't mind spending. Nobody knows about men's ways better than we do. Sunday and Monday is the Derby-day like, and then after that they are about cracked up and done. The largest amount I've taken at Southwark on a Sunday is eighty – over £4 worth, but then in the week-days it's different; Sunday's fifteen shillings we think that very tidy, some days only three or four shillings.

You see we are obliged to resort to all sort of dodges to make sixpenny portraits pay. It's a very neat little picture our sixpenny ones is; with a little brass rim round them, and a neat metal inside, and a front glass; so how can that pay if you do the legitimate business? The glass will cost you twopence a-dozen – this small size – and you give two with every picture; then the chemicals will cost quite a halfpenny, and varnish, and frame, and fittings, about twopence. We reckon threepence out of each portrait. And then you see there's house-rent and a man at the door, and boy at the table, and the operator, all to pay their wages out of this sixpence; so you may guess where the profit is.

One of our dodges is what we term 'An American Air-Preserver', which is nothing more than a card – old benefit tickets, or, if we are hard up, even brown paper, or anythink – soap wrappings, just varnished on one side. Between our private residence and our shop, no piece of card or old paper escapes us. Supposing a party come in, and says 'I should like a portrait'; then I inquire which they'll have, a shilling or a sixpenny one. If they prefer a sixpenny one, I then make them one up, and I show them one of the air-preservers – which we keep ready made up – and I tell them that they are all chem-icalised, and come from America, and that without them their picture will fade. I also tell them that I make nothing out of them, for that they are only twopence and cost all the money; and that makes 'em buy one directly. They always bite at them; and we've actually had people come to us to have our preservers put upon other persons' portraits, saying they've been everywhere for them and can't get them. I charge threepence if it's not one of our pictures. I'm the original in-ventor of the 'Patent American Air-Preserver'. We first called them the 'London Air-Preservers' but they didn't go so well as since they've been the Americans.

Another dodge is, I always take the portrait on a shilling size; and after they are done, I show them what they can have for a shilling – the full size, with the knees; and table and a vase on it – and let them understand that for sixpence they have all the back-ground and legs cut off; so as many take the shilling portraits as sixpenny ones.

Talking of them preservers, it is astonishing how they go. We've actually had photographers themselves come to us to buy our 'American Air-Preservers'. We tells them it's a secret, and we manufacture them ourselves. People won't use their eyes. Why, I've actually cut up an old band-box afore the people's eyes, and varnished it and dried it on the hob before their eyes, and yet they still fancy they come from America! Why, we picks up the old paper from the shop-sweeping, and they make first-rate 'Patent American Air-Preservers'. Actually, when we've been short, I've torn off a bit of old sugar-paper, and stuck it on without any varnish at all, and the party has gone away quite happy and contented. But you must remember it is really a useful thing, for it does do good and do preserve the picture.

Another of our dodges – and it is a splendid dodge, though it wants a nerve to do it – is the brightening solution, which is nothing more than aqua distilled, or pure water. When we take a portrait, Jim, my mate, who stops in the room, hollows to me, 'Is it bona?' That is, is it good? If it is, I say, 'Say'. That is, Yes. If not, I say 'Nanti'. If it is a good one he takes care to publicly expose that one, that all may see it, as a recommendation to others. If I say 'Nanti', then Jim takes it and finishes it up, drying it and putting it up in its frame. Then he wraps it up in a large piece of paper, so that it will take some-time to unroll it, at the same time crying out 'Take sixpence from this lady, if you please.' Sometimes she says, 'O let me see it first'; but he always answers, 'Money first, if you please ma'am; pay for it first, and then you can do what you like with it. Here, take sixpence from this lady.' When she sees it, if it is a black one, she'll say, 'Why this ain't like me; there's no picture at all.' Then Jim says, 'It will become better as it dries, and come to your natural complexion.' If she still grumbles, he tells her that if she likes to have it passed through the brightening solution, it will come out lighter in an hour or two. They in general have it brightened; and then, before their face, we dip it into some water. We then dry it off and replace it in the frame, wrap it up carefully, and tell them not to expose it to the air, but put it in their bosom, and in an hour or two it will be all right. This is only done when the portrait come out black, as it doesn't pay to take two for sixpence. Sometimes they brings them back the next day, and says, 'It's not dried out as you told us'; and then we take another portrait, and charge them threepence more.

We also do what we call the 'bathing' – another dodge. Now today a party came in during a shower of rain, when it was so dark it was impossible to take a portrait; or they will come in, sometimes, just as we are shutting up, and when the gas is lighted, to have their portraits taken; then we do this. We never turn business away, and yet it's impossible to take a portrait; so we ask them to sit down, and then we go through the whole process of taking a portrait, only we don't put any plate in the camera. We always make 'em sit a long time, to make 'em think it's all right – I've had them for two-and-a-half minutes, till their eyes run down with water. We then tell them that we've taken the portrait, but that we shall have to keep it all night in the chemical bath to bring it out, because the weather's so bad. We always take the money as a deposit, and give them a written paper as an order for the picture. If in the morning they come themselves we get them to sit again, and then we do really take a portrait of them; but if they send anybody, we either say that the bath was too strong and eat the picture out, or that it was too weak and didn't bring it out; or else I blow up Jim, and pretend he has upset the bath and broke the picture. We have had as many as ten pictures to bathe in one afternoon.

If the eyes in a portrait are not seen, and they complain, we take a pin and dot them; and that brings the eye out, and they like it. If the hair, too, is not visible we takes the pin again, and soon puts in a beautiful head of hair. It requires a deal of nerve to do it; but if they still grumble I say, 'It's a beautiful picture, and worth half-a-crown, at the least'; and in the end they generally go off contented and happy.

When we are not busy, we always fill up the time taking specimens for the window. Anybody who'll sit we take him; or we do one another, and the young woman in the shop who colours. Specimens are very useful things to us, for this reason, – if anybody comes in a hurry, and won't give us time to do the picture, then, as we can't afford to let her go, we sit her and goes through all the business, and I says to Jim, 'Get one from the window,' and then he takes the first specimen that comes to hand. Then we fold it up in paper, and don't allow her to see it until she pays for it, and tell her not to expose it to the air for three days, and that if then she doesn't approve of it and will call again we will take her another. Of course they in general comes back. We have made some queer mistakes doing this. One day a young lady came in, and wouldn't wait, so Jim takes a specimen from the window, and, as luck would have it, it was the portrait of a widow in her cap. She insisted upon opening, and then she said, 'This isn't me; it's got a widow's cap, and I was never married in all my life!' Jim answers, 'Oh, miss! why it's a beautiful picture, and a correct likeness,' – and so it was, and no lies, but it wasn't of her. Jim talked to her, and says he, 'Why this ain't a cap, it's the shadow of the hair – for she had ringlets – and she positively took it away believing that such was the case; and even promised to send us customers, which she did.

There was another lady that came in a hurry, and would stop if we were not more than a minute; so Jim ups with a specimen, without looking at it, and it was the picture of a woman and her child. We went through the business of focussing the camera, and then gave her the portrait and took the sixpence When she saw it she cries out, 'Bless me! there's a child: I haven't ne'er a child!' Jim looked at her, and then at the picture, as if comparing, and says he, 'It is certainly a wonderful likeness, miss, and one of the best we ever took. It's the way you sat; and what has occasioned it was a child passing through the yard.' She said she supposed it must be so, and took the portrait away highly delighted.

Once a sailor came in, and as he was in haste, I shoved on to him the picture of a carpenter, who was to call in the afternoon for his portrait. The jacket was dark, but there was a white waistcoat; still I persuaded him that it was his blue Guernsey which had come up very light, and he was so pleased that he gave us ninepence instead of sixpence. The fact is, people don't know their own faces. Half of 'em have never looked in a glass half a dozen times in their life, and directly they see a pair of eyes and a nose, they fancy they are their own.

The only time we were done was with an old woman. We had only one specimen left, and that was a sailor man, very dark – one of our black pictures. But she put on her spectacles, and she looked at it up and down, and says, 'Eh?' I said, 'Did you speak, ma'am?' and she cries, 'Why, this is a man! here's the whiskers.' I left, and Jim tried to humbug her, for I was bursting with laughing. Jim said, 'It's you ma'am; and a very excellent likeness, I assure you.' But she kept on saying, 'Nonsense, I ain't a man,' and wouldn't have it. Jim wanted her to leave a deposit, and come next day, but she never called. It was a little too strong.

There was an old woman come in once and wanted to be taken with a favourite hen in her lap. It was a very bad picture, and so black there was nothing but the outline of her face and a white speck for the beak of the bird. When she saw it, she asked where the bird was? So Jim took a pin and scratched in an eye, and said, 'There it is, ma'am – that's her eye, it's coming out,' and then he made a line for the comb on the head, and she kept saying, 'Wonderful!' and was quite delighted.

The only bad money we have taken was from a Methodist clergyman, who came in for a one shilling and sixpence portrait. He gave us a bad sixpence.

For colouring we charge threepence more. If the portraits are bad or dark we tell them, that if they have them coloured the likeness will be perfect. We flesh the face, scratch the eye in, and blue the coat and colour the tablecloth. Sometimes the girl who does it puts in such a lot of flesh paint, that you can scarcely distinguish a feature of the person. If they grumble, we tell them it will be all right when the picture's dry. If it's a good picture, the colour looks very nice, but in the black ones we are obliged to stick it on at a tremendous rate, to make it show.

Jim stands at the door, and he keeps on saying, 'A correct portrait, framed and glazed, for sixpence, beautifully enamelled.' Then, when they are listening, he shows the specimen in his hands, and adds, 'If not approved of, no charge made.'

One morning, when we had been doing 'quisby,' that is, stopping idle, we hit upon another dodge. Some friends dropped in to see me, and as I left to accompany them to a tavern close by, I cried to Jim, 'Take that public-house opposite.' He brought the camera and stand to the door, and a mob soon collected. He kept saying, 'Stand back, gentlemen, stand back! I am about to take the public-house in front by this wonderful process.' Then he went over to the house, and asked the landlord, and asked some gentlemen drinking there to step into the road whilst he took the house with them facing it. Then he went to a policeman and asked him to stop the carts from passing, and he actually did. By this way he got up a tremendous mob. He then put in the slide, pulled off the cap of the camera, and focussed the house, and pretended to take the picture, though he had no prepared glass, nor nothing. When he had done, he called out, 'Portraits taken in one minute. We are now taking portraits for sixpence only. Time of sitting, two seconds only. Step inside and have your'n taken immediately.' There was a regular rush, and I had to be fetched, and we took six shillings worth right off.

People seem to think the camera will do anything. We actually persuade them that it will mesmerise them. After their portrait is taken, we ask them if they would like to be mesmerised by the camera, and the charge is only twopence. We then focus the camera, and tell them to look firm at the tube; and they stop there for two or three minutes staring, till their eyes begin to water, and then they complain of a dizziness in the head, and give it up, saying they 'can't stand it'. I always tell them the operation was beginning, and they were just going off, only they didn't stay long enough. They always remark, 'Well, it certainly is a wonderful machine, and a most curious invention.' Once a coalheaver came in to be mesmerised, but he got into a rage after five or six minutes, and said, 'Strike me dead, ain't you keeping me a while!' He wouldn't stop still, so Jim told him his sensitive nerves was too powerful, and sent him off cursing and swearing because he couldn't be mesmerised. We don't have many of these mesmerism customers, not more than four in these five months; but it's a curious circumstance, proving what fools people is. Jim says he only introduces these games when business is dull, to keep my spirits up – and they certainly are most laughable.

I also profess to remove warts, which I do by touching them with nitric acid. My price is a penny a wart, or a shilling for the job; for some of the hands is pretty well smothered with them. You see, we never turn money away, for it's hard work to make a living at sixpenny portraits. My wart patients seldom come twice, for they screams out ten thousand blue murders when the acid bites them.

Another of my callings is to dye the hair. You see I have a good many refuse baths, which is mostly nitrate of silver, the same as all hair-dyes is composed of. I dyes the whiskers and moustache for a shilling. The worst of it is, that nitrate of silver also blacks the skin wherever it touches. One fellow with carroty hair came in one day to have his whiskers dyed, and I went clumsily to work and let the stuff trickle down his chin and on his cheeks, as well as making the flesh at the roots as black as a hat. He came the next day to have it taken off, and I made him pay threepence more, and then removed it with cyanide, which certainly did clean him, but made him smart awfully.

I have been told that there are near upon 250 houses in London now getting a livelihood taking sixpenny portraits. There's ninety of 'em I'm personally acquainted with, and one man I know has ten different shops of his own. There's eight in the Whitechapel-road alone, from Butcher-row to the Mile-end turnpike. Bless you, yes! They all make a good living at it. Why, I could go tomorrow, and they would be glad to employ me at £2 a-week – indeed they have told me so.

If we had begun earlier this summer, we could, only with our little affair, have made from £8 to £10 a-week, and about one-third of that is expenses. You see, I operate myself, and that cuts out £2 a-week.[40]

Chapter Six: Homes and Residents

Although many of the people Mayhew spoke to were inter-viewed at their work in streets and workshops, he often made some effort to see people's homes, where he had the chance to meet wives and children. No detail was too small to report if it gave some extra understanding of the lives of poor Londoners. The state of clothes and furniture, the body language of resi-dents, even small items of decoration or ornament bring to life the characters of people as well as their living conditions.

There was a significant Irish population in London in the mid-eighteenth century, many driven out of their homeland by the Potato Famine, and with his eye for accuracy, Mayhew often tried to reproduce their speech. He described in some detail the importance of religion in their lives, as we see in this account of the homes of the street Irish.

I visited one of the paved yards round which the Irish live, and found that it had been turned into a complete drying-ground, with shirts, gowns, and petticoats of every description and colour. The buildings at the end were completely hidden by 'the things', and the air felt damp and chilly, and smelt of soap-suds. The gutter was filled with dirty gray water emptied from the wash-tubs, and on the top were the thick bubbles floating about under the breath of the boys 'playing at boats' with them.

It is the custom with the inhabitants of these courts and alleys to assemble at the entrance with their baskets, and chat and smoke away the morning. Every court entrance has its little group of girls and women, lolling listlessly against the sides, with their heads uncovered, and their luxuriant hair fuzzy as oakum. It is peculiar with the Irish women that – after having been accustomed to their hoods – they seldom wear bonnets, unless on a long journey. Nearly all of them, too, have a thick plaid shawl, which they keep on all the day through, with their hands covered under it. At the mouth of the only thoroughfare deserving of the name of street – for a cart could just go through it – were congregated about thirty men and women, who rented rooms in the houses on each side of the road. Six women, with baskets of dried herrings, were crouching in a line on the kerb-stone with the fish before them; their legs were drawn up so closely to their bodies that the shawl covered the entire figure, and they looked very like the podgy 'tombolers' sold by the Italian boys. As all their wares were alike, it was puzzling work to imagine how, without the strongest opposition, they could each obtain a living. The men were dressed in long-tail coats, with one or two brass buttons. One old dame, with a face wrinkled like a dried plum, had her cloak placed over her head like a hood, and the grisly hair hung down in matted hanks about her face, her black eyes shining between the locks like those of a Skye terrier; beside her was another old woman smoking a pipe so short that her nose reached over the bowl.

After looking at the low foreheads and long bulging upper lips of some of the group, it was pleasant to gaze upon the pretty faces of the one or two girls that lolled against the wall. Their black hair, smoothed with grease, and shining almost as if 'japanned', and their large gray eyes with the thick dark fringe of lash, seemed out of place among the hard features of their companions. It was only by looking at the short petticoats and large feet you could assure yourself that they belonged to the same class.

In all the houses that I entered were traces of household care and neatness that I had little expected to have seen. The cupboard fastened in the corner of the room, and stocked with mugs and cups, the mantelpiece with its images, and the walls covered with showy-coloured prints of saints and martyrs, gave an air of comfort that strangely disagreed with the reports of the cabins in 'ould Ireland'. As the doors to the houses were nearly all of them kept open, I could, even whilst walking along, gain some notion of the furniture of the homes. In one house that I visited there was a family of five persons, living on the ground floor and occupying two rooms. The boards were strewn with red sand, and the front apartment had three beds in it, with the printed curtains drawn closely round. In a dark room, at the back, lived the family itself. It was fitted up as a parlour, and crowded to excess with chairs and tables, the very staircase having pictures fastened against the wooden partition. The fire, although it was midday, and a warm autumn morning, served as much for light as for heat, and round it crouched the mother, children, and visitors, bending over the flame as if in the severest winter time. In a room above this were a man and woman lately arrived in England. The woman sat huddled up in a corner smoking, with the husband standing over her in, what appeared at first, a menacing attitude; I was informed, however, that they were only planning for the future. This room was perfectly empty of furniture, and the once white-washed walls were black, excepting the little square patches which showed where the pictures of the former tenants had hung. In another room, I found a home so small and full of furniture, that it was almost a curiosity for domestic management. The bed, with its chintz curtains looped up, filled one end of the apartment, but the mattress of it served as a long bench for the visitors to sit on. The table was so large that it divided the room in two, and if there was one picture there must have been thirty – all of 'holy men', with yellow glories round their heads. The window-ledge was dressed out with crockery, and in a tumbler were placed the beads. The old dame herself was as curious as her room. Her shawl was fastened over her large frilled cap. She had a little 'button' of a nose, with the nostrils entering her face like bullet holes. She wore over her gown an old pilot coat, well-stained with fish slime, and her petticoats being short, she had very much the appearance of a Dutch fisherman or stage smuggler.

Her story was affecting – made more so, perhaps, by the emotional manner in which she related it. Nine years ago 'the father' of the district – 'the Blissed Lady guard him!' – had found her late at night, rolling in the gutter, and the boys pelting her with orange-peel and mud. She was drunk – 'the Lorrud pass by her' – and when she came to, she found herself in the chapel, lying before the sanctuary, 'under the shadow of the holy cross'. Watching over her was the 'good father', trying to bring back her consciousness. He spoke to her of her wickedness, and before she left she took the pledge of temperance. From that time she prospered, and the one and sixpence the 'father' gave her 'had God's blissin' in it', for she became the best dressed woman in the court, and in less than three years had £15 in the savings' bank, 'the father – Heaven cherish him' – keeping her book for her, as he did for other poor people. She also joined 'the Association of the Blissed Lady', (and bought herself the dress of the order 'a beautiful grane vilvit, which she had now, and which same cost her thirty shillings'), and then she was secure against want in old age and sickness. But after nine years' prudence and comfort, a brother of hers returned home from the army, with a pension of a shilling a day. He was wild, and persuaded her to break her pledge, and in a short time he got all her savings from her and spent every penny. She couldn't shake him off, 'for he was the only kin she had on airth', and 'she must love her own flish and bones'. Then began her misery. 'It plased God to visit her ould limbs with aches and throubles, and her hips swole with the cowld,' so that she was at last forced into a hospital, and all that was left of her store was 'aten up by sufferins'. This, she assured me, all came about by the 'good father's' leaving that parish for another one, but now he had returned to them again, and, with his help and God's blessing, she would yet prosper once more.

Whilst I was in the room, the father entered, and 'old Norah', half-divided between joy at seeing him and shame at 'being again a beggar', laughed and wept at the same time. She stood wiping her eyes with the shawl, and groaning out blessings on 'his rivirince's hid', begging of him not 'to scould her for she was a wake woman'. The renegade brother was had in to receive a lecture from 'his rivirince'. A more sottish idiotic face it would be difficult to imagine. He stood with his hands hanging down like the paws of a dog begging, and his two small eyes stared in the face of the priest, as he censured him, without the least expression even of consciousness. Old Norah stood by, groaning like a bagpipe, and writhing while the father spoke to her 'own brother', as though every reproach were meant for her.

The one thing that struck me during my visit to this neighbourhood, was the apparent listlessness and lazy appearance of the people. The boys at play were the only beings who seemed to have any life in their actions. The women in their plaid shawls strolled along the pavements, stopping each friend for a chat, or joining some circle, and leaning against the wall as though utterly deficient in energy. The men smoked, with their hands in their pockets, listening to the old crones talking, and only now and then grunting out a reply when a question was directly put to them. And yet it is curious that these people, who here seemed as inactive as negroes, will perform the severest bodily labour, undertaking tasks that the English are almost unfitted for.[41]

Wherever there was a main road in London that had to be crossed by pedestrians, there would be a bevy of crossing-sweepers, essential particularly in wet weather to clear a path through mud and horse manure. Crossing-sweepers could be of all ages, but because the job required little skill, they attracted elderly or disabled people as well as young children. One day, Mayhew asked two boy crossing-sweepers, called Harry and 'the Goose' if he could see where they lived.

The boys led me in the direction of Drury-lane; and before entering one of the narrow streets which branch off like the side-bones of a fish's spine from that long thoroughfare, they thought fit to caution me that I was not to be frightened, as nobody would touch me, for all was very civil.

The locality consisted of one of those narrow streets which, were it not for the paved cartway in the centre would be called a court. Seated on the pavement at each side of the entrance was a costerwoman with her basket before her, and her legs tucked up mysteriously under her gown into a round ball, so that her figure resembled in shape the plaster tumblers sold by the Italians. These women remained as inanimate as if they had been carved images, and it was only when a passenger went by that they gave signs of life, by calling out in a low voice, like talking to themselves, 'Two for three haarpence – herrens'; 'Fine hinguns'.

The street itself is like the description given of thoroughfares in the East. Opposite neighbours could not exactly shake hands out of window, but they could talk together very comfortably; and, indeed, as I passed along, I observed several women with their arms folded up like a cat's paws on the sill, and chatting with their friends over the way.

Nearly all the inhabitants were costermongers, and, indeed, the narrow cartway seemed to have been made just wide enough for a truck to wheel down it. A beershop and a general store, together with a couple of sweeps – whose residences were distinguished by a broom over the door – formed the only exceptions to the street-selling class of inhabitants.

As I entered the place, it gave me the notion that it belonged to a distinct coster colony, and formed one large hawkers' home; for everybody seemed to be doing just as he liked, and I was stared at as if considered an intruder. Women were seated on the pavement, knitting, and repairing their linen; the door-ways were filled up with bonnetless girls, who wore their shawls over their head, as the Spanish women do their mantillas; and the youths in corduroy and brass buttons, who were chatting with them, leant against the walls as they smoked their pipes, and blocked up the pavement, as if they were the proprietors of the place. Little children formed a convenient bench out of the kerbstone; and a party of four men were seated on the footway, playing with cards which had turned to the colour of brown paper from long usage, and marking the points with chalk upon the flags.

The parlour-windows of the houses had all of them wooden shutters, as thick and clumsy-looking as a kitchen flap-table, the paint of which had turned to the dull dirt colour of an old slate. Some of these shutters were evidently never used as a security for the dwelling, but served only as tables on which to chalk the accounts of the day's sales.

Before most of the doors were costermongers' trucks – some standing ready to be wheeled off, and others stained and muddy with the day's work. A few of the costers were dressing up their barrows, arranging the sieves of waxy-looking potatoes – and others taking the stiff herrings, browned like a meerschaum with the smoke they had been dried in, from the barrels beside them, and spacing them out in pennyworths on their trays.

You might guess what each costermonger had taken out that day by the heap of refuse swept into the street before the doors. One house had a blue mound of mussel-shells in front of it – another, a pile of the outside leaves of broccoli and cabbages, turning yellow and slimy with bruises and moisture.

Hanging up beside some of the doors were bundles of old strawberry pottles, stained red with the fruit. Over the trap-doors to the cellars were piles of market-gardeners' sieves, ruddled like a sheep's back with big red letters. In fact, everything that met the eye seemed to be in some way connected with the coster's trade.

From the windows poles stretched out, on which blankets, petticoats, and linen were drying; and so numerous were they, that they reminded me of the flags hung out at a Paris fête. Some of the sheets had patches as big as trap-doors let into their centres; and the blankets were – many of them – as full of holes as a pigeon-house.

As I entered the court, a 'row' was going on; and from a first-floor window a lady, whose hair sadly wanted brushing, was haranguing a crowd beneath, throwing her arms about like a drowning man, and in her excitement thrusting her body half out of her temporary rostrum as energetically as I have seen Punch lean over his theatre.

'The villain dragged her,' she shouted, 'by the hair of her head, at least three yards into the court – the villain! And then he kicked her, and the blood was on his boot.'

It was a sweep who had been behaving in this cowardly manner; but still he had his defenders in the women around him. One with very shiny hair, and an Indian kerchief round her neck, answered the lady in the window, by calling her a 'damned old cat'; whilst the sweep's wife rushed about, clapping her hands together as quickly as if she was applauding at a theatre, and styled somebody or other 'an old wagabones as she wouldn't dirty her hands to fight with'.

This 'row' had the effect of drawing all the lodgers to the windows – their heads popping out as suddenly as dogs from their kennels in a fancier's yard.

The room where the boys lodged was scarcely bigger than a coach-house; and so low was the ceiling, that a fly-paper suspended from a clothes-line was on a level with my head, and had to be carefully avoided when I moved about.

One corner of the apartment was completely filled up by a big four-post bedstead, which fitted into a kind of recess as perfectly as if it had been built to order.

The old woman who kept this lodging had endeavoured to give it a homely look of comfort, by hanging little black-framed pictures, scarcely bigger than pocket-books, on the walls. Most of these were sacred subjects, with large yellow glories round the heads; though between the drawing representing the bleeding heart of Christ, and the Saviour bearing the Cross, was an illustration of a red-waistcoated sailor smoking his pipe. The Adoration of the Shepherds, again, was matched on the other side of the fireplace by a portrait of Daniel O'Connell.

A chest of drawers was covered over with a green baize cloth, on which books, shelves, and clean glasses were tidily set out.

Where so many persons (for there were about eight of them, including the landlady, her daughter, and grandson) could all sleep, puzzled me extremely.

The landlady wore a frilled nightcap, which fitted so closely to the skull, that it was evident she had lost her hair. One of her eyes was slowly recovering from a blow, which, to use her own words, 'a blackgeyard gave her'. Her lip, too, had suffered in the encounter, for it was swollen and cut.

'I've a nice flock-bid for the boys,' she said, when I inquired into the accommodation of her lodging-house, 'where three of them can slape aisy and comfortable.'

'It's a large bed, sir,' said one of the boys, 'and a warm covering over us; and you see it's better than a regular lodging-house; for, if you want a knife or a cup, you don't have to leave something on it till it's returned.'

The old woman spoke up for her lodgers, telling me that they were good boys, and very honest; 'For,' she added, 'they pays me rig'lar ivery night, which is threepence.'

The only youth as to whose morals she seemed to be at all doubtful was 'the Goose', 'for he kept late hours, and sometimes came home without a penny in his pocket'.

A little girl, who worked by herself at her own crossing, had a peculiarly flat face, with a button of a nose, while her mouth was scarcely larger than a button-hole. When she spoke, there was not the slightest expression visible in her features; indeed, one might have fancied she wore a mask and was talking behind it; but her eyes were shining the while as brightly as those of a person in a fever, and kept moving about, restless with her timidity. The green frock she wore was fastened close to the neck, and was turning into a kind of mouldy tint; she also wore a black stuff apron, stained with big patches of gruel, 'from feeding baby at home', as she said. Her hair was tidily dressed, being drawn tightly back from the forehead, like the buy-a-broom girls; and as she stood with her hands thrust up her sleeves, she curtseyed each time before answering, bobbing down like a float, as though the floor under her had suddenly given way.[42]

We've seen how Mayhew observes tiny details of the surroundings in the homes of the people he met, from holy pictures to dirt-encrusted walls or curtains. He inferred the characters of people from the state of their homes and also from the nature of their hobbies, as in this comment on the difference between bird-owners and dog-owners.

The readers who have perused this work from its first appearance will have noticed how frequently I have had to comment on the always realized indication of good conduct, and of a superior taste and generally a superior intelligence, when I have found the rooms of working people contain flowers and birds. I could adduce many instances. I have seen and heard birds in the rooms of tailors, shoemakers, coopers, cabinetmakers, hatters, dress-makers, curriers, and street-sellers – all people of the best class. One of the most striking, indeed, was the room of a street confectioner. His family attended to the sale of the sweets, and he was greatly occupied at home in their manufacture, and worked away at his peppermint-rock, in the very heart of one of the thickliest populated parts of London, surrounded by the song of thrushes, linnets, and goldfinches, all kept, not for profit, but because he 'loved' to have them about him. I have seldom met a man who impressed me more favourably.

The flowers in the room are more attributable to the super-intending taste of a wife or daughter, and are found in the apartments of the same class of people.

There is a marked difference between the buyers or keepers of birds and of dogs in the working classes, especially when the dog is of a sporting or 'varmint' sort. Such a dog-keeper is often abroad and so his home becomes neglected; he is interested about rat-hunts, knows the odds on or against the dog's chance to dispatch his rats in the time allotted, loses much time and customers, his employers grumbling that the work is so slowly executed, and so custom or work falls off. The bird-lover, on the other hand, is generally a more domestic, and, perhaps consequently, a more prosperous and contented man. It is curious to mark the refining qualities of particular trades. I do not remember seeing a bulldog in the possession of any of the Spitalfields silk-weavers: with them all was flowers and birds. The same I observed with the tailors and other kindred occupations. With slaughterers, however, and drovers, and Billingsgatemen, and coachmen, and cabmen, whose callings naturally tend to blunt the sympathy with suffering, the gentler tastes are comparatively unknown. The dogs are almost all of the 'varmint' kind, kept either for rat-killing, fighting, or else for their ugliness. For 'pet' or 'fancy' dogs they have no feeling, and in singing birds they find little or no delight.[43]

A significant proportion of Mayhew's 500 or so interviewees would have seen better days. Some came down in the world because of illness, others because of bad luck and the lack of a welfare safety net other than the much-abhorred workhouse. One of the homes he visited was that of a former clerk in a government office who was now trying to get work as a dock labourer to support his wife and children.

He lived in a top back-room in a small house, in another dismal court. I was told by the woman who answered the door to mount the steep stairs, as she shrieked out to the man's wife to show me a light. I found the man seated on the edge of a bed, with six young children grouped round him. They were all shoeless, and playing on the bed was an infant with only a shirt to cover it. The room was about seven feet square, and, with the man and his wife, there were eight human creatures living in it. In the middle of the apartment, upon a chair, stood a washing-tub foaming with fresh suds, and from the white crinkled hands of the wife it was plain that I had interrupted her in her washing. On one chair, close by, was a heap of dirty linen, and on another was flung the newly-washed. There was a saucepan on the handful of fire, and the only ornaments on the mantelpiece were two flat-irons and a broken shaving-glass. On the table at which I took my notes there was the bottom of a broken ginger-beer bottle filled with soda. The man was without a coat, and wore an old tattered and greasy black satin waistcoat. Across the ceiling ran strings to hang clothes upon. On my observing to the woman that I supposed she dried the clothes in that room, she told me that they were obliged to do so, and it gave them all colds and bad eyes. On the floor was a little bit of matting, and on the shelves in the corner one or two plates. In answer to my questionings the man told me he had been a dock-labourer for five or six years. He was in Her Majesty's Stationery Office. When there he had £150 a-year. Left through accepting a bill of exchange for £871. He was suspended eight years ago, and had petitioned the Lords of the Treasury, but never could get any answer. After that he was out for two or three years, going about doing what he could get, such as writing letters. 'Then,' said the wife, 'you went into M. What's-his-name's shop.' 'Oh, yes,' answered the man, 'I had six months' employment at Camberwell. I had twelve shillings a-week and my board there.'

Before this they had lived upon their things. He had a good stock of furniture and clothing at that time. The wife used to go out for a day's work when she could get it. She used to go out shelling peas in the pea season – washing or charing – anything she could get to do. His father was a farmer, well to do. He should say the old man was worth a good bit of money, and he would have some property at his death.

'Oh, sir,' said the woman, 'we have been really very bad off indeed; sometimes without even food or firing in the depth of winter. It is not until recently that we have been to say very badly off, because within the last four years has been our worst trouble. We had a very good house – a seven-roomed house in Walworth – and well furnished and very comfortable. We were in business for ourselves before we went there. We were grocers, near Oxford-street. We lived there at the time when Aldis the pawnbroker's was burnt down. We might have done well if we had not given so much credit.'

'I've got,' said the husband, 'about £90 owing me down there now. It's quite out of character to think of getting it. At Clerkenwell I got a job at a grocer's shop. The master was in the

Queen's-bench Prison, and the mistress employed me at twelve shillings a-week until he went through the Insolvent Debtor's Court. When he passed the Court the business was sold, and of course he didn't want me after that. I've done nothing else but this dock labouring work for this long time. Took to it first because I found there was no chance of anything else. The character with the bill transaction was very much against me: so, being unable to obtain employment in a wholesale house, or anywhere else, I applied to the docks. They require no character at all there. I think I may sometimes have had seven or eight days altogether. Then I was out for a fortnight or three weeks perhaps; and then we might get a day or two again, and on some occasion such a thing as – well, say July, August, September, and October. I was in work one year almost the whole of those months – three years ago I think that was. Then I did not get anything, excepting now and then, not more than about three days' work until the next March; that was owing to the slack time. The first year I might say that I might have been employed about one-third of the time. The second year I was employed six months. The third year I was very unfortunate. I was laid up for three months with bad eyes and a quinsey in the throat, through working in an ice ship. I've scarcely had anything to do since then. That is nearly eighteen months ago; and since then I have had casual employment, perhaps one, and sometimes two days a-week. It would average five shillings a-week the whole year. Within the last few weeks I have, through a friend, applied at a shipping-merchant's, and within the month I have had five days' work with them, and nothing else, except writing a letter, which I had twopence for that's all the employment I've met with myself. My wife has been at employment for the last three months, she has a place she goes to work at. She has three shillings a-week for washing, for charing, and for mangling: the party my wife works for has a mangle, and I go sometimes to help; for if she has got sixpence worth of washing to do at home, than I go to turn the mangle for an hour instead of her – she's not strong enough.'

'We buy most bread,' said the wife, 'and a bit of firing, and I do manage on a Saturday night to get them a bit of meat for Sunday if I possibly can; but what with the soap, and one thing and another, that's the only day they do get a bit of meat, unless I've a bit given me. As for clothing, I'm sure I can't get them any unless I have that given me, poor little things.'

'Yes, but we have managed to get a little bread lately,' said the man. 'When bread was elevenpence a loaf, that was the time when we was worse off. Of course we had the seven children alive then. We buried one only three months ago. She was an afflicted little creature for sixteen or seventeen months: it was one person's work to attend to her, and was very badly off for a few months then. We've known what it was sometimes to go without bread and coals in the depth of winter. Last Christmas two years we did so for the whole day, until the wife came home in the evening and brought it might be sixpence or ninepence according how long she worked. I was looking after them. I was at home ill. I have known us to sit several days and not have more than sixpence to feed and warm the whole of us for the whole of the day. We'll buy half-a-quartern loaf, that'll be fourpence halfpenny or sometimes fivepence, and then we have a penny for coals, that would be pretty nigh all that we could have for our money. Sometimes we get a little oatmeal and make gruel. We had hard work to keep the children warm at all. What with their clothes and what we had, we did as well as we could. My children is very contented; give'em bread, and they're as happy as all the world. That's one comfort. For instance, to-day we've had half a quartern loaf, and we had a piece left of last night's after I had come home. I had been earning some money yesterday. We had two ounces of butter, and I had this afternoon a quarter of an ounce of tea and a pennyworth of sugar. When I was ill I've had two or three of the children round me at a time, fretting for want of food. That was at the time I was ill. A friend gave me half a sovereign to bury my child. The parish provided me with a coffin, and it cost me about three shillings besides. We didn't have her taken away from here, not as a parish funeral exactly. I agreed that if he would fetch it, and let it stand in an open space that he had got there, near his shop, until the Saturday, which was the time, I would give the undertaker three shillings to let a man come with a pall to throw over the coffin, so that it should not be seen exactly it was a parish funeral. Even the people in the house don't know, not one of them, that it was buried in that way. I had to give one shilling and sixpence for a pair of shoes before I could follow my child to the grave, and we paid one and ninepence for rent, all out of the half sovereign. I think there's some people at the docks a great deal worse off than us. I should say there's men go down there and stand at that gate from seven to twelve, and then they may get called in and earn a shilling, and that only for two or three days in the week, after spending the whole of their time there.'[44]

Not every house Mayhew visited presented scenes of squalor and deprivation. One of Mayhew's preoccupations was the toll which drink took of the lives of people in its grip. One particular group of labourers, coal-heavers, had managed to break free of the automatic payment of wages via the local pubkeeper, who made sure that significant amounts of earnings were taken in drink rather than cash. When Mayhew visited the home of one of these men, he found a very different scene from that which he had witnessed in many poor homes.

I found the whole family assembled in the back kitchen that served them for a parlour. As I entered the room the mother was busy at work, washing and dressing her children for the day. There stood six little things, so young that they seemed to be all about the same height, with their faces shining with the soap and water, and their cheeks burning red with the friction of the towel. They were all laughing and playing about the mother, who, with comb and brush in hand, found it no easy matter to get them to stand still while she made 'the parting'. First of all the man asked me to step upstairs and see the sleeping-room. I was much struck with the scrupulous cleanliness of the apartment. The blind was as white as snow, half rolled up, and fastened with a pin. The floor was covered with patches of different coloured carpet, showing that they had been bought from time to time, and telling how difficult it had been to obtain the luxury. In one corner was a cupboard with the door taken off, the better to show all the tumblers, teacups, and coloured-glass mugs, that, with two decanters, well covered with painted flowers, were kept more for ornament than use. On the chimneypiece was a row of shells, china shepherdesses, and lambs, and a stuffed pet canary in a glass-case for a centre ornament. Against the wall, surrounded by other pictures, hung a half-crown watercolour drawing of the wife, with a child on her knee, matched on the other side by the husband's likeness, cut out in black paper. Pictures of bright-coloured ducks and a print of Father Moore, the teetotaler, completed the collection.

'You see,' said the man, 'we manages pretty well; but I can assure you we has a hard time of it to do it at all comfortably. Me and my wife is just as we stands – all our other things are in pawn. If I was to drink I don't know what I should do. How others manage is to me a mystery. This will show you I speak the truth,' he added, and going to a secretary that stood against the wall he produced a handful of duplicates. There were seven-teen tickets in all, amounting to three pounds and sixpence, the highest sum borrowed being ten shillings. 'That'll show you

I don't like my poverty to be known, or I should have told you of it before. And yet we manage to sleep clean'; and he pulled back the patchwork counterpane, and showed me the snow-white sheets beneath. 'There's not enough clothes to keep us warm, but at least they are clean. We're obliged to give as much as we can to the children. Cleanliness is my wife's hobby, and I let her indulge in it. I can assure you last week my wife had to take the gown off her back to get a shilling on it. My little ones seldom have a bit of meat from one Sunday to another, and never a bit of butter.'

I then descended into the parlour. The children were all seated on little stools that their father had made for them in his spare moments, and warming themselves round the fire, their little black shoes resting on the white hearth. From their regular features, small mouths, large black eyes, and fair skins, no one would have taken them for a labouring man's family. In answer to my questions, he said: 'The eldest of them (a pretty little half-clad girl, seated in one corner) is ten, the next seven, that one five, that three, and this (a little thing perched upon a table near the mother) two. I've got all their ages in the Bible upstairs.' I remarked a strange look about one of the little girls. 'Yes, she always suffered with that eye; and down at the hospital they lately performed an operation on it.' An artificial pupil had been made.

The room was closed in from the passage by a rudely built partition. 'That I did myself in my leisure,' said the man, 'it makes the room snugger.' As he saw me looking at the clean rolling-pin and bright tins hung against the wall, he observed: 'That's all my wife's doing. She has got them together by some-times going without dinner herself, and laying out the twopence or threepence in things of that sort. That is how she manages. Today she has got us a sheep's head and a few turnips for our Sunday's dinner,' he added, taking off the lid of the boiling saucepan. Over the mantelpiece hung a picture of George IV, surrounded by four other frames. One of them contained merely three locks of hair. The man, laughing, told me, 'Two of them are locks of myself and my wife, and the light one in the middle belonged to my wife's brother, who died in India. That's her doing again,' he added.[45]

Phrases worthy of Dickens appear in these passages: the woman with 'a little "button" of a nose, with the nostrils entering her face like bullet holes'; the man who 'stood with his hands hanging down like the paws of a dog begging' while Old Norah 'stood by, groaning like a bagpipe'. Then there's the tongue-in-cheek remark about the husband who stood 'in what appeared at first, a menacing attitude; I was informed, however, that they were only planning for the future'.

And what a vivid picture is conveyed by the description of the argument in the street: 'As I entered the court, a "row" was going on; and from a first-floor window a lady, whose hair sadly wanted brushing, was haranguing a crowd beneath, throwing her arms about like a drowning man, and in her excitement thrusting her body half out of her temporary rostrum as energetically as I have seen Punch lean over his theatre.'

Chapter Seven: 'Our Pet Thief'

In spite of a huge amount of what would be called today 'multi-tasking' – writing for the Morning Chronicle, *writing novels, editing magazines, running campaigns – Mayhew had a full and lively home life. Occasionally, as in the episode entitled 'Our Pet Thief', we get glimpses both of what that life was like and of how his sympathy for the ne'er-do-wells could impinge on his own family life.*

On one of his visits to talk to the young residents of what he called 'low lodging-houses' Mayhew met a boy who seemed redeemable from a life of petty crime, and so he tried to redeem him. The meeting is described as follows.

I sought to find out how many among the number had been confined in prison. 'I've been in quod, sir, I have,' cried one. 'I've been in, too,' shouted a second. And finding the answers to come too quickly for me to take down, I requested those who had been inmates of a gaol to hold up their hands. They did so, and I counted eighteen out of the twenty-nine who were my companions. 'Ah, there's quite that,' said the best-looking man of the party; 'If the whole twenty-nine of us was down, it would not be too much, I'm sure.' The young beggar-boy here advanced again to me, and with a knowing wink, cried, 'I can't tell how many times I've been in – oh! it's above counting. I'm sure it's above a dozen times.' I wished to see the size of the farthing's worth of coffee and sugar that they had spoken of as constituting their meals, and I spoke to the gentleman who had brought me to the place as to the possibility of getting a sample of the quantity. He directed me to give one of the boys a shilling, saying the lad would fetch what I wanted. Seeing that I hesitated doing as be requested, he took one from his purse, and giving it to a lad of the name of Dan, whose physiognomy was not of the most prepossessing description, he told him to go for what I wished. The boy quitted the room, and I must confess I never expected to see him enter it again. I now asked the lodgers the reason why they preferred theft to work. 'We don't,' was the answer; 'It's precious hard work having to walk the street, I can tell you; but we can't get nothing to do.' 'Look at me,' cried one standing up. The man was literally a mass of rags and filth. His tattered clothes and shirt were black and shiny as a sailor's dreadnought with grease and dirt. 'Look at me; who'd give me a day's work in the state I am! Why, the best job I've had I only got threepence by, and I don't make above two and sixpence a week honestly at the outside. We couldn't live on what we get, and yet we can live on a precious little here. Get a meal for five farthings. A farthing's worth of coffee, a farthing's worth of sugar, and half a pound of bread, three farthings. We can have a slap-up dinner for two-pence; a common one for a penny.' 'Oh, yes, a regular roarer for two-pence!' cried the beggar boy. 'Three halfpenny-worth of pudding, and a halfpenny-worth of gravy.' 'Or else we can have,' said another, '2½ lb. of taturs – that's a penny – and ½ lb. fourpenny bacon – that's another penny. That's what we calls a first-rate dinner. Very often we're forced to put up with a penn'orth of taturs and a halfpenny herring – that's a three-halfpenny dinner. There's a chap here was forced to do today with a ha'p'orth of taturs. He's been out ever since, and perhaps won't come in at all tonight. He'll walk the streets and starve.' At this point the boy came back with the farthing's worth of coffee and sugar, and to my utter astonishment produced the elevenpence halfpenny of change. He was without shirt to his back or shoe to his foot, and when I asked him whether he had ever been in prison, he told me he had been 'quodded' three times for vagrancy, and once on suspicion of highway robbery! I expressed my surprise at the honesty of the young thief. 'Why, there's not a chap among them that wouldn't have done the same thing,' said my companion, who knew their characters well; 'they would all have done the same, except that one smoking there,' pointing to an ill-looking lad in a Scotch cap. 'When you gave me the shilling,' cried Dan, 'he followed me into the yard, and told me to hook it.' I whispered with my companion as to whether it were possible to take the poor shoeless boy, who had resisted this double temptation, from the wretched and demoralizing associations of the place, and make an honest man of him. 'No,' was his answer; 'He is hopeless. This is the chivalry of these people. Make friends of them, and they will scarcely ever deceive you. They may be trusted with pounds by those whom they know; but as for industry or getting an honest living, it's out of the question. I have known a few in my time that have been reclaimed, but they are the exceptions, and certainly not the rule.'[46]

In spite of the firm discouragement of his informant, Mayhew apparently decided to take Dan into his own home to see if the experience of a very different sort of home life would reform him. He later wrote about the experience in the Comic Almanac, *a* Punch-*like humour magazine. Although the piece is written as by his wife, it is likely that it was Mayhew himself who wrote it, with a certain amount of comic licence but surely several grains of truth:*

In making some inquiries relative to the state of the criminal population, my husband found it necessary to visit a low lodging-house, the abode of thieves and pickpockets. He there became acquainted with 'Dan', and (from his returning some money that was given him to change) took such a fancy to him, that he determined to try whether the lad, who had resisted the temptation (for he could have gone off with the money with great ease), could not – if taken from his wretched and demoralizing associates – be induced to withstand all other temptations.

The boy (for he was but fourteen years of age), on being questioned, expressed a wish to change his mode of living, and he was brought home to me. When my husband told me what motives he had in taking charge of the lad, I must confess that in the impulse of the moment I thought it a worthy thing to do; for in my innocence I imagined that all thieves merely wanted some one to take them by the hand to put them in the way of getting an honest living.

In the evening we talked over a variety of plans for the boy's reformation. He was to be sent to school and well educated. There were many good men to be found, we were convinced, that would feel proud to take charge of him; and when he left school we were to put him to some trade or other. I really believe, in our own minds, we imagined that we should live to see him a great man! Who knew but that he might one day be Lord Mayor of London; stranger things than that, we both agreed, had occurred to poor boys. That he would ever return to his evil practices appeared to us impossible, if we would but look upon him as the good member of society that we wished him to become.

Little, alas! did we then know of the annoyance and trouble our 'Pet Thief' would cause us!

The appearance of the poor shoeless creature was anything but prepossessing. His cheek-bones were high; his hair was cut close on the top, with a fringe of locks, as it were, left hanging in front; and he wore an old plaid shooting-jacket, that was black and shining with grease, and fastened together with pieces of string.

The first thing to be done was to make him take a bath. He had a great horror of washing, and seemed to look upon it as quite a barbarism. Some clothes were got together by subscription among the members of the family – one contributing a coat, another a pair of boots, and so on; but he looked, I think, worse in our things than he did in his own. The coat reached his heels, and was so large (my husband being corpulent) that the boy had difficulty in keeping in it.

We arranged that he should sleep out of the house, so we hired a bed-room for him at a coffee-shop in the neighbourhood. I thought I could find him work in the house by day, and so keep him employed under our own eyes, and prevent his returning to his old practices and companions until we could get him into some school. Anything for change: his disposition and previous mode of life forbade his remaining in one place, or at the same occupation, for any length of time.

The third morning after his coming to us, while we were at breakfast, Dan entered the room, and requested, in a most mysterious manner, to speak with my husband. He was told that he was quite at liberty to communicate what he had to say before the family; but he pointed to me, and replied, 'I don't want to speak afore *her*,' so I quitted the apartment. As soon as I had gone, the boy told my husband that he *must* get him to buy him a small-tooth comb; his head was in such a dreadful state, he said, that he thought he had better have one directly. When my husband informed me of the object of the mysterious visit, I felt cold all over; for I remembered how close I had sat to him during the lessons the previous day. Then I thought of the children, and began to repent of ever having admitted such a person into the house.

But this was only the beginning of my annoyances with the boy. My husband thought it would be a good 'moral lesson' for our children to let them know that Dan had been a thief, and that he had been in prison a great many times; but that he had resolved to become a good boy, and that was our reason for having him with us. This, however, instead of having the effect intended, made the children look upon Dan as an object of great interest, so much so, indeed, that they were always wanting, whenever they saw him, to ask him something about the prison, 'whether the policeman had really taken him away, and whether it was true he had only bread and water in gaol?'

One morning, on going downstairs, I discovered (to my great horror) our little boy, with his mouth wide open, seated on Dan's knee, listening most attentively to some story. Upon questioning the child I found that our 'pet pickpocket' had been telling the little fellow of the fun it was to go 'sawney hunting', which I afterwards learnt was stealing pieces of bacon from shop doors.

The Sunday evening after this the cook, who was naturally timid, had been left at home with Dan alone, it being the other maid's 'Sunday out'. They were both sitting very comfortably talking by the fire-light (for it was winter time) when Master Dan thought fit to tell the girl all about his previous life. He gave her some very vivid illustrations of housebreaking, and informed her that Sunday night, when the family had gone to church, was their best time. He also told her of the many times that he had been in Newgate, and that once he had been taken up on 'suspicion' of highway robbery; it was an old woman he helped to rob, and he told of the 'lark' they had with her, and of how they had left her with her hands and feet tied together in a ditch.

All these stories so terrified the poor girl that she felt convinced that the boy meant to take advantage of the tranquillity of that Sunday evening, 'their best time', to serve her as he had done the 'old woman'; so she rushed to the street door in her fright, and there we found her on our return home, crying and in a dreadful state of excitement. She vowed that she would quit the house the very next morning, and she wondered how we could leave her with a 'common pickpocket'. I tried to quiet her (for she was a very good girl, and I did not wish to part with her), by telling her that we wished to reform the lad; but nothing would pacify her save his leaving the house; so I told my husband that he must really find a school for the boy, or we should be left without servants.

He accordingly went in search of a school. It was wonderful to see how anxious the masters were to have the youth, until my husband informed them (for it was considered but right to do so) that the boy he wished to introduce to them as a pupil had lately been an inmate of Newgate. On hearing this they invariably assured him that there was a school 'just up the street' that was the very thing he wanted. Upon visiting the establishment 'just up the street', however, he found the master was astonished that the 'head' of such a school as the previous one should refer my husband to him, for he was sure that Mr —'s school was the very place for such boys – nevertheless, as Mr — had refused to take the lad, there was an academy a short distance from that establishment that, he was sure, would not shut their doors against him. But upon going there it was the old story over again, and we soon discovered that it was impossible to find any respectable establishment willing to take charge of our young thief.

We were at last obliged to give up all idea of getting him into any school, so we thought the best thing to be done was to try and find him a situation. In the meantime he got tired of the work he was directed to do, and would sit all day long looking at the fire without taking the least notice of any one; and if told that he should occupy himself in some way or other, he would turn sullen, and mutter something between his teeth about his being promised to be put to school, and why wasn't he sent to school when that was all he wanted?

I found that my meat began to disappear in a most mysterious manner. One day the half of a goose went no one knew where. I suspected Dan; my husband was indignant (for he wished to think the boy had forgotten his bad habits), and said, 'It was easy for the servants to make out that Dan had purloined it.' This annoyed me so much that I did not hesitate to tell my husband that I saw clearly we should have no peace in the house until the boy was provided with a situation out of it.

At last the long-looked-for situation was found. It was at a large wholesale stationer's. The proprietor was made acquainted with the boy's whole history, and he promised to do all he could to effect his reformation. But upon Dan's going to him, the gentleman was so taken aback by the boy's expression, that he sent a polite note stating 'That he should really be afraid, from his looks, to have such a character in his establishment.'

In a few days afterwards he was on his way to America.

The last we heard of him was that he and several 'reformed criminals' from the London ragged schools were 'working' (as the thieves call it) the city of New York. In conclusion, it is but right I should add that, although the boy while with us was frequently trusted with money to change, he never defrauded us of a sixpence.[47]

Chapter Eight: Uses of Literacy

There are two unintended but very valuable consequences of Mayhew's interests and technique. Firstly, his accurate steno-graphic records of what people actually said – even allowing for the occasional smoothing out that comes with removing his own voice from the material – give us an almost phonographic account of how people spoke, something we find very rarely in any other writings of the time. Dickens could, of course, repro-duce the speech mannerisms of a whole range of different classes, but when he made Sam Weller say 'There; now we look compact and comfortable, as the father said ven he cut his little boy's head off, to cure him o' squintin', Weller didn't actually say anything, never had and never would, since he didn't exist. But each of the people Mayhew met was a real person and spoke in a way that reflected the education and culture of his or her class. We have seen this time and again in the extracts quoted so far. There almost certainly was a lad of fourteen selling muffins and he almost certainly did say, at some point: 'I turns out with muffins and crumpets, sir, in October, and continues until it gets well into the spring, according to the weather. I carries a fust-rate article; werry much so. If you was to taste 'em, sir, you'd say the same.'

But the second unintended consequence of Mayhew's omnivo-rous curiosity was the insight it gives us now into the popular culture of Londoners and in particular their appetite for 'stories', either through reading books, newspapers or periodicals, or by listening to street reciters and patterers. Look, for example, at the range and nature of books that were available in the street bookstalls.

The street book-stalls are most frequent in the thoroughfares which are well-frequented, but which, as one man in the trade expressed himself, are not so 'shoppy' as others – such as the City-road, the New-road, and the Old Kent-road. 'If there's what you might call a recess,' observed another street book-stall-keeper, '*that's* the place for us; and you'll often see us along with flower-stands and pinners-up.' The stalls themselves do not present any very smart appearance; they are usually of plain deal. If the stock of books be sufficiently ample, they are disposed on the surface of the stall, 'fronts up', as I heard it described, with the titles, when lettered on the back, like as they are presented in a library. If the 'front' be unlettered, as is often the case with the older books, a piece of paper is attached, and on it is inscribed the title and the price. Sometimes the description is exceeding curt, as, 'Poetry', 'French', 'Religious', 'Latin' (I saw an odd volume, in Spanish, of Don Quixote, marked 'Latin', but it was at a shop-seller's stall), 'Pamphlets', and such like; or where it seems to have been thought necessary to give a somewhat fuller appellation, such titles are written out as 'Locke's Understanding', 'Watts's Mind', or 'Pope's Rape'. If the stock be rather scant, the side of the book is then shown, and is either covered with white paper, on which the title and price are written, or 'brushed', or else a piece of paper is attached, with the necessary announcement.

Sometimes these announcements are striking enough, as where a number of works of the same size have been bound together (which used to be the case, I am told, more frequently than it is now); or where there has been a series of stories in one volume. One such announcement was, 'Smollett's Peregrine Pickle Captain Kyd Pirate Prairie Rob of the Bowl Bamfyeld Moore Carew 2*s*.' Alongside this miscellaneous volume was, 'Wilberforce's Practical View of Christianity, 1*s*.', 'Fenelon's Aventures de Télémaque, plates, 9*d*.', 'Arres, de Predestinatione, 1*s*.' (the last-mentioned work, which, at the first glance, seems as if it were an odd mixture of French and Latin, was a Latin quarto), 'Coronis ad Collationem Hagiensem, &c. &c., Gulielmo Amesio.' Another work, on another stall, had the following description: 'Lord Mount Edgecumbe's Opera What is Currency Watts's Scripture History Thoughts on Taxation only 1s. 3d.' Another was, 'Knickerbocker Bacon 1s.' As a rule, however, the correctness with which the work is described is rather remarkable.

At some few of the street-stalls, and at many of the shop-stalls, are boxes, containing works marked, 'All 1d.' or 2d., 3d., or 4d. Among these are old Court-guides, Parliamentary Companions, Railway Plans, and a variety of sermons, and theological, as well as educational and political pamphlets. To show the character of the publications thus offered – not, perhaps, as a rule, but generally enough, for sale – I copied down the titles of some at a penny and twopence.

All these at 1d.: 'Letters to the Right Honourable Lord John Russell, on State Education, by Edward Baines, jun.'; 'A Pastoral Letter to the Clergy and Members of the Protestant Episcopal Church in the United States of America'; 'A Letter to the Protestant Dissenters of England and Wales, by the Rev. Robert Ainslie'; 'Friendly Advice to Conservatives'; 'Elementary Thoughts on the Principles of Currency and Wealth, and on the Means of Diminishing the Burdens of the People, by J. D. Basset, Esq., price 2s. 6d.' The others were each published at a shilling.

All these at 2d.: 'Poems, by Eleanor Tatlock, 1811, 2 vols., 9s.'; 'Two Sermons, on the Fall and Final Restoration of the Jews, by the Rev. John Stuart'; 'Thoughts and Feelings, by Arthur Brooke, 1820'; 'The Amours of Philander and Sylvia, being the third and last part of Love-letters between a Nobleman and his Sister. Volume the Second. The Seventh Edition. London.'

From a cursory examination of the last-mentioned twopenny volume, I could see nothing of the nobleman or his sister. It is one of an inane class of books, originated, I believe, in the latter part of the reign of Charles II. Such publications professed to be (and some few were) records of the court and city scandal of the day, but in general they were works founded on the reputation of the current scandal. In short, to adopt the language of patterers, they were 'cocks' issued by the publishers of that period; and they continued to be published until the middle of the eighteenth century, or a little later. I notice this description of literature the more, particularly as it is still frequently to be met with in street-sale. 'There's oft enough,' one street-book-seller said to me, 'works of that sort making up a "lot" at a sale, and in very respectable rooms. As if they were make weights, or to make up a sufficient number of books, and so they keep their hold in the streets.'[48]

Running patterers were men who walked the street with printed accounts – often fictional, when they were called 'cocks' – of events in the news. At the period Mayhew was recording these interviews there were several major stories for which the public seemed to have an insatiable appetite. Not surprisingly, a grue-some murder followed by a trial and an execution made good copy, and if the patterer had scant access to the actual details he made the stuff up. The account includes a certain amount of gentle editorializing by Mayhew, who compares the graphic and often made-up details hawked about by the patterers with the accounts of the same crimes given in the newspapers of the time read by people of a higher social class but, in Mayhew's view, just as sensationalist.

Some of the names that crop up in the following account of running patterers need a little explanation: Feargus O'Connor was Irish MP in the British parliament, a radical and a leading Chartist, eventually certified as a lunatic; Louis Napoleon was a nephew of Napoleon Bonaparte, who spent some time in exile in England until 1848, when he returned to France and was elected president; Marshal Haynau was a brutal Hungarian general whose exploits in struggles with European revolutionaries included whipping women who sympathized with the rebels, and hanging thirteen generals of the revolutionary cause. On a visit to London he was attacked and beaten by draymen of a brewery he was visiting; 'Rush' was James Blomfield Rush, a tenant farmer who murdered the family of the owner of the estate; Jane Wilbred was a servant girl cruelly treated by her employers, Mr and Mrs Sloane; 'Manning' was Marie Manning, convicted with her husband of the murder of her lover, and executed together; 'Good' was Daniel Good, a coachman who murdered his girlfriend and, when questioned by a constable, locked the man in a stable with his victim's body; 'Oxford' was Edward Oxford who, aged eighteen, fired a shot at Queen Victoria, was tried, found guilty, and sent to Bedlam.

If the truth be saleable, a running patterer prefers selling the truth, for then – as one man told me – he can 'go the same round comfortably another day'. If there be no truths for sale – no stories of criminals' lives and loves to be condensed from the diffusive biographies in the newspapers – no 'helegy' for a great man gone – no prophecy and no crim. con. – the death hunter invents, or rather announces, them. He puts some one to death for the occasion, which is called 'a cock'. The paper he sells may give the dreadful details, or it may be a religious tract, 'brought out in mistake', should the vendor be questioned on the subject; or else the poor fellow puts on a bewildered look and murmurs, 'O, it's shocking to be done this way – but I can't read.' The patterers pass along so rapidly that this detection rarely happens.

One man told me that in the last eight or ten years, he, either singly or with his 'mob', had twice put the Duke of Wellington to death, once by a fall from his horse, and the other time by a 'sudden and mysterious' death, without any condescension to particulars. He had twice performed the same mortal office for Louis Phillipe, before that potentate's departure from France; each death was by the hands of an assassin; 'One was stabbing, and the other a shot from a distance.' He once thought of poisoning the Pope, but was afraid of the street Irish. He broke Prince Albert's leg, or arm (he was not sure which), when his royal highness was out with his harriers. He never had much to say about the Queen; 'It wouldn't go down,' he thought, and perhaps nothing had lately been said. 'Stop, there, sir,' said another patterer, of whom I inquired as to the correctness of those statements (after my constant custom in sifting each subject thoroughly), 'stop, stop, sir. I *have* had to say about the Queen lately. In course, nothing can be said against her, and nothing ought to; that's true enough, but the last time she was confined, I cried her *accouchement* (the word was pronounced as spelt to a merely English reader, or rather more broadly) of *three!* Lord love you, sir, it would have been no use crying *one;* people's so used to that; but a Bobby came up and he stops me, and said it was some impudence about the Queen's *coachman!* Why look at it, says I, fat-head – I knew I was safe – and see if there's anything in it about the Queen or her coachman! And he looked, and in course there was nothing. I forget just now what the paper *was* about.'

My first-mentioned informant had apprehended Feargus O'Connor on a charge of high treason. He assassinated Louis Napoleon 'from a *fourth* edition of the *Times*' which 'did well'. He caused Marshal Haynau to die of the assault by the draymen. He made Rush hang himself in prison. He killed Jane Wilbred, and put Mrs Sloane to death; and he announced the discovery that Jane Wilbred was Mrs Sloane's daughter.

This informant did not represent that he had originated these little pieces of intelligence, only that he had been a party to their sale, and a party to originating one or two. Another patterer and of a higher order of genius told me that all which was stated was undoubtedly correct, 'But me and my mates, sir,' he said, 'did Haynau in another style. A splendid slum, sir! Capital! We assassinated him – mysterious. Then about Rush. His hanging hisself in prison was a fake, I know; but we've had him lately. His ghost appeared – as is shown in the Australian papers – to Emily Sandford, and threatened her; and took her by the neck, and there's the red marks of his fingers to be seen on her neck to this day!' The same informant was so loud in his praise of the 'Ass-sass-sination' of Haynau that I give the account. I have little doubt it was his own writing. It is confused in passages, and has a blending of the 'I' and the 'we':

> We have just received upon undisputed authority, that, that savage and unmanly tyrant, that enemy to civil and religious liberty, the inhuman Haynau has at last finished his career of guilt by the hand of an assassin, the term assassin I have no doubt will greet harshly upon the ears of some of our readers, yet never the less I am compelled to use it although I would gladly say the *average* of outraged innocence, which would be a name more suitable to one who has been the means of ridden the world of such a despicable monster.

My informant complained bitterly, and not without reason, of the printer. 'Average', for instance (which I have italicised) should be 'avenger'. 'The "average of outraged innocence!"'

'It appears by the Columns of the Corour le Constituonal of Brussels,' runs the paper,

> that the evening before last, three men one of which is supposed to be the miscreant, Haynau entered a Cafe in the Neighbourhood of Brussels kept by a man in the name of

Priduex, and after partaking of some refreshments which were ordered by his two companions they desired to be shown to their chambers, during their stay in the public or Travellers Room, they spoke but little and seemed to be very cautious as to joining in the conversations which was passing briskly round the festive board, which to use the landlord's own words was rather strange, as his Cafe was mostly frequented by a set of jovial fellows, M. Priduex goes on to state that after the three strangers had retired to rest some time a tall and rather noble looking man enveloped in a large cloak entered and asked for a bed, and after calling for some wine he took up a paper and appeared to be reading it very attentively, in due time he was shown to bed and all passed on without any appearance of anything wrong until about 6 o'clock in the morning, when the landlord and his family, were roused by a noise over head and cries of murder, and upon going up stairs to ascertain the cause, he discovered the person who was [known] to be Marshal Haynau, lying on his bed with his throat cut in a frightful manner, and his two companions standing by his bed side bewailing his loss. On the table was discovered a card, on which was written these words 'Monster, I am avenged at last.' Suspicion went upon the tall stranger, who was not anywhere to be found, the Garde arms instantly were on the alert, and are now in active persuit of him but up to the time of our going to press nothing further has transpired.

It is very easy to stigmatise the death-hunter when he sets off all the attractions of a real or pretended murder – when he displays on a board, as does the standing patterer, 'illustrations' of 'the ''dentical pick-axe' of Manning, or the stable of Good – or when he invents or embellishes atrocities which excite the public mind. He does, however, but follow in the path of those who are looked up to as 'the press' – as the 'fourth estate'. The conductors of the *Lady's Newspaper* sent an artist to Paris to give drawings of the scene of the murder by the Duc de Praslin, – to 'illustrate' the bloodstains in the duchess's bed-chamber. The *Illustrated London News* is prompt in depicting the locality of any atrocity over which the curious in crime may gloat. The *Observer,* in costly advertisements, boasts of its twenty columns (sometimes with a supplement) of details of some vulgar and mercenary bloodshed – the details being written in a most honest deprecation of the morbid and savage tastes to which the writer is pandering. Other weekly papers have engravings – and only concerning murder – of any wretch whom vice has made notorious. Many weekly papers had expensive telegraphic despatches of Rush's having been hung at Norwich, which event, happily for the interest of Sunday newspapers, took place in Norwich at noon on a Saturday. (I may here remark, that the patterers laugh at telegraphs and express trains for rapidity of communication, boasting that the press strives in vain to rival *them* – as at a 'hanging match', for instance, the patterer has the full particulars, dying speech, and confession included – if a confession be feasible – ready for his customers the moment the drop falls, and while the criminal may still be struggling, at the very scene of the hanging. At a distance he sells it before the hanging. 'If the *Times* was cross-examined about it,' observed one patterer, 'he must confess he's outdone, though he's a rich *Times,* and we is poor fellows.' But to resume –

A penny-a-liner is reported, and without contradiction, to have made a large sum by having hurried to Jersey in Manning's business, and by being allowed to accompany the officers when they conducted that paltry tool of a vindictive woman from Jersey to Southampton by steamer, and from Southampton to London by 'special engine', as beseemed the popularity of so distinguished a rascal and homicide; and next morning the daily papers, in all the typographical honour of 'leads' and 'a good place', gave details of this fellow's – this Manning's – conversation, looks, and demeanour.

Until the 'respectable' press become a more healthful public instructor, we have no right to blame the death-hunter, who is but an imitator – a follower – and that for a meal. So strong has this morbid feeling about criminals become, that an earl's daughter, who had 'an order' to see Bedlam, would not leave the place until she had obtained Oxford's autograph for her album! The rich vulgar are but the poor vulgar – without an excuse for their vulgarity.

'Next to murders, fires are tidy browns,' I was told by a patterer experienced both in 'murders' and 'fires'. The burning of the old Houses of Parliament was very popular among street-sellers, and for the reason which ensures popularity to a commercial people; it was a source of profit, and was certainly made the most of. It was the work of incendiaries, of ministers, to get rid of perplexing papers, of government officers with troublesome accounts to balance, of a sporting lord, for a heavy wager, of a conspiracy of builders, and of 'a unsuspected party'. The older 'hands' with whom I conversed on the subject, all agreed in stating that they 'did well' on the fire. One man said, 'No, sir, it wasn't only the working people that bought of me, but merchants and their clerks. I s'pose they took the papers home with 'em for their wives and families, which is a cheap way of doing, as a newspaper costs threepence at least. But stop, sir, stop; there wasn't no threepennies then, nothing under six-pence, if they wasn't more; I can't just say, but it was better for us when newspapers was high. I never heard no sorrow expressed, not *in* the least. Some said it was a good job, and they wished the ministers was in it.' The burning of the Royal Exchange was not quite so beneficial to the street-sellers, but 'was uncommon tidy'.[49]

A higher cultural tone was set by young men who walked the streets reciting verse and drama for money. Mayhew had some trouble finding any of these to talk to but persisted and found some to visit in their rooms in the City.

There were two of them – one a lad, who was dressed in a man's ragged coat and burst boots, and tucked-up trowsers, and seemingly in a state of great want; and the other decently enough attired in a black paletot with a flash white-and-red handkerchief, or 'fogle' as the costermongers call it, jauntily arranged so as to bulge over the closely-buttoned collar of his coat. There was a priggish look about the latter lad, while his manner was 'cute', and smacked of Petticoat-lane; and though the other one seemed to slink back, he pushed himself saucily forward, and at once informed me that he belonged 'to the profession' of street declaimer. 'I and this other boy goes out together,' he said, as he took a short pipe from his mouth; and in proof of his assertion, he volunteered that they should on the spot give me a specimen of their histrionic powers.

I preferred listening to the modest boy. He was an extremely good-looking lad, and spoke in a soft voice, almost like a girl's. He had a bright, cheerful face, and a skin so transparent and healthy, and altogether appeared so different from the generality of street lads, that I felt convinced that he had not long led a wandering life, and that there was some mystery connected with his present pursuits. He blushed when spoken to, and his answers were nervously civil.

When I had the better-natured boy alone with me, I found that he had been well educated; and his statement will show that he was born of respectable parents, and the reason why he took to his present course of life. At first he seemed to be nervous, and little inclined to talk; but as we became better acquainted, he chatted on even faster than my pen could follow.

He had picked up several of the set phrases of theatrical parlance, such as, 'But my dream has vanished in air'; or, 'I felt that a blight was on my happiness'; and delivered his words in a romantic tone, as though he fancied he was acting on a stage. He volunteered to show me his declamatory powers, and selected 'Othello's Apology'. He went to the back of the room, and after throwing his arms about him for a few seconds, and looking at the ceiling as if to inspire himself, he started off.

Whilst he had been chatting to us his voice was – as I said before – like a girl's; but no sooner did he deliver his, 'Most potent, grave, and reverend Signiors,' than I was surprised to hear him assume a deep stomachic voice – a style evidently founded upon the melodramatic models at minor theatres. His good-looking face, however, became flushed and excited during the delivery of the speech, his eyes rolled about, and he passed his hands through his hair, combing it with his fingers till it fell wildly about his neck like a mane.

When he had finished the speech he again relapsed into his quiet ways, and resuming his former tone of voice, seemed to think that an apology was requisite for the wildness of his acting, for he said, 'When I act Shakespeare I cannot restrain myself – it seems to master my very soul.'

He had some little talent as an actor, but was possessed of more memory than knowledge of the use of words. Like other performers, he endeavoured to make his 'points' by dropping his voice to almost a whisper when he came to the passage, 'I, faith 'twas strange, 'twas passing strange.'

In answer to my questions he gave me the following statement.

I am a street reciter, that is, I go about the streets and play Shakespeare's tragedies, and selections from poets. The boys in the streets call me Shakespeare. The first time they called me so I smiled at them, and was honoured by the name, though it's only passing! it's only fleet!

I was born in Dublin, and my father was in the army, and my mother was a lady's nurse and midwife, and used to go out on urgent business, but only to ladies of the higher classes. My mother died in Dublin, and my father left the army and became a turnkey in Dublin prison. Father left Dublin when I was about ten years of age, and went to Manchester. Then I went into an office – a herring-store, which had agents at Yarmouth and other fishing-ports; and there I had to do writing. Summer-time was our busiest time, for we used to have to sit up at night waiting for the trains to come in with the fish. I used to get threepence an hour for every hour we worked over, and sixpence in the morning for coffee, and eight and sixpence standing wages, whether I worked or played. I know all about herrings and herring-packing, for I was two years there, and the master was like a father to me, and would give me money many times, Christmas-boxes, and new-years' gifts, and such-like. I might have been there now, and foreman by this time, in the Isle of Man, where we had a house, only I was too foolish – going to theatres and such-like.

You see, I used, before I went out as clerk, to go to a school in Manchester, where the master taught recitation. We used to speak pieces from Uwin's 'Elocution', and we had to get a piece off to elocution, and attitude, and position; indeed, elocution may be said to be position and attitude. We used to do 'The Downfall of Poland', and 'Lord Ullen's Daughter', and 'My name is Norval', and several others – 'Rolla', and all them. Then we used to speak them one at a time, and occasionally we would take different parts, such as the 'Quarrel of Brutus', and 'Cassius', and 'Rolla', and the 'American Patriot', and such-like. I will not boast of myself, but I was one of the best in the class, though since I have gone out in the streets it has spoiled my voice and my inclinations, for the people likes shouting. I have had as many as 500 persons round me in the Walworth-road at one time, and we got four shillings between us; and then we lost several halfpence, for it was night, and we could not see the money that was thrown into the ring. We did the 'Gipsy's Revenge', and 'Othello's Apology'.

Whilst I was at the herring-stores I used to be very fond of the theatre, and I'd go there every night if I could, and I did nearly manage to be there every evening. I'd save up my money, and if I'd none I'd go to my master and ask him to let me have a few halfpence; and I've even wanted to go to the play so much that, when I couldn't get any money, I'd sell my clothes to go. Master used to caution me, and say that the theatre would ruin me, and I'm sure it has. When my master would tell me to stop and do the books, I'd only just run them over at night and cast them up as quickly as I could, and then I'd run out and go to the twopenny theatre on the Victoria-bridge, Manchester. Sometimes I used to perform there for Mr Row, who was the proprietor. It was what is called a travelling 'slang', a booth erected temporarily. I did William Tell's son, and I've also done the 'Bloody Child' in Macbeth, and go on with the witches. It was a very little stage, but with very nice scenery, and shift-scenes and all, the same as any other theatre. On a Saturday night he used to have as many as six houses; start off at three o'clock, after the factory hands had been paid off. I never had any money for acting, for though he offered me half-a-sovereign a-week to come and take a part, yet I wouldn't accept of it, for I only did it for my own amusement like. They used to call me King Dick.

My master knew I went to the theatre to act, for he sent one of the boys to follow me, and he went in front and saw me acting in Macbeth, and he went and told master, because, just as the second act was over, he came right behind the scenes and ordered me out, and told me I'd have to get another situation if I went there any more. He took me home and finished the books, and the next morning I told him I'd leave, for I felt as if it was my sole ambition to get on to the stage, or even put my foot on it; I was so enamoured of it. And it is the same now, for I'd do anything to get engaged – it's as if a spell was on me. Just before I left he besought me to remain with him, and said that I was a useful hand to him, and a good boy when I liked, and that he wanted to make a gentleman of me. He was so fond of me that he often gave me money himself to go to a theatre; but he said too much of it was bad.

After I left him I went with another boy to go to sea. I forgot all about the theatre, for it agitated my feelings when I left him, and I wished I had been back, for I'd been with him eighteen months, and he'd been like a father to me; but I was too ashamed to see him again. This boy and me started for Scarborough, and he had no money, and I had five shillings that was all between us; but I had a black suit of clothes cost two pounds ten shillings, which my master had made me a present of, for excelling the foreman in making up the books – for the foreman was 208 hands of herrings (five herrings make a hand) short in one week; and then I took the books the next week, and I was only four herrings short, and master was so pleased that he bestowed upon me a present of a new suit of clothes.

I parted with my companion for this reason. One day, after we had been walking, we were so hungry we could eat any-thing, and I had been accustomed to never being hungry, so that I was very much exhausted from fatigue, for we had walked thirty miles that day, only eating one piece of bread, which I got at a public-house where I gave a recitation. We came to a farm-house at a place called Bishop Wilton, in Yorkshire, and he went inside the door to beg for something to eat. There was a young lady came out and talked to him and gave him some bread, and then she saw me and had compassion on me, because I looked respectable and was so miserable. We told her we were cousins, and had left our fathers and mothers (for we didn't like to say we had left our masters), and she said, 'Poor boys! your parents will be fretting after you; I'd go back, if I was you.' She gave him a large bit of bread, and then she gave me a big bit of cold plum-pudding. My companion wanted half my pudding besides his own bread, and I preferred to give him part of the pudding and not have any bread; but he wouldn't, and struck out at me. I returned it, and then we fought, and an old woman came out with a stick and beat us both, and said we were incorrigible young beggars, and couldn't be very hungry or we shouldn't fight that way. Then I parted from my companion, and he took the direct road to Scarborough, and I went to York. I saw him afterwards when I returned to Manchester. His father left him £200, and he's doing very well in a good situation in a commercial office.

I got bound for six years to sea to a shipowner at Scarborough, but the mate behaved very bad to me and used me brutally. I couldn't use the ropes as well as he thought I might, although I learned the compass and all the ropes very soon. The captain was a very good man, but I daren't tell him for fear of the mate. He used to beat me with the rope's end – sometimes the lead-rope – that was his usual weapon, and he used to leave marks on me. I took the part of Hamlet, and, instead of complaining, I thought of that part where he says,

And makes us rather bear those ills we have,
Than fly to others that we know not of.

That's the best play of Shakespeare; he outdoes himself there.

When the brig got to Scheidam, in Holland, five miles off Rotterdam, I ran away. The vessel was a collier, and whilst they were doing the one, two, three, and pulling up the coals, I slipped over the side and got to shore. I walked to Rotterdam, and there I met an Irish sailor and told him all, and he told me to apply to the British Consul and say that I had been left ashore by a Dutch galliot, which had sailed the day before for Jersey. The Consul put me in a boarding-house – a splendid place, with servants to wait on you, where they gave me everything, cigars and all, for everybody smokes there – little boys scarce higher than the table – and cigars are only a cent each – and five cents make a penny. I was like a gentleman then, and then they put me in the screw steamer, the Irwell, and sent me back to Hull.

When I got to Manchester again, I went in my sailor-clothes to see my old master. He was very glad to see me, and asked me if I wanted anything to eat, and sent out for ale for me, and was so glad to see me that he gave me money. He took me back again at higher wages, ten shillings – which was one and sixpence over – and I stopped there eight months, until they wrote to me from Dublin that father was very ill, and that I was to come over directly. So I went, and was by him when he died. He was sixty-two years of age, and left £400 to my sister, which she is to have when she comes of age. He quarrelled with me because he was a Catholic, and I didn't follow that persuasion, and he disowned me; but, just before he died, he blessed me, and looked as if he wanted to say something to me, but he couldn't, for the breath was leaving him.

When I returned to Manchester I found my master had taken another servant, as he expected I should stop in Dublin, and there was no vacancy; but he recommended me to another merchant, and there I was put in the yard to work among the herrings, as he didn't know my capabilities; but, in a short time I was put in the shop as boy, and then I was very much in favour with the master and the missus, and the son, and he used to bring me to concerts and balls, and was very partial to me; and I used to eat and drink with them at their own table. I've been foolish, and never a friend to myself, for I ran away from them. A lad told me that London was such a fine place, and induced me to sell my clothes and take the train; and here I've been for about eight months knocking about.

As long as my money lasted I used to go to the theatre every night – to the Standard, and the City-road, and the Britannia; but when it was gone I looked then to see what I might do. At first I tried for a situation, but they wouldn't take me, because I couldn't get a recommendation in London. Then I formed a resolution of giving recitations from Shakspeare and the other poets in public-houses, and getting a living that way.

I had learned a good deal of Shakespeare at school; and besides, when I was with my master I had often bought penny copies of Shakespeare, and I used to study it in the office, hiding it under the book I was writing in; and, when nobody was looking, studying the speeches. I used to go and recite before the men in the yard, and they liked it.

The first night I went out I earned four shillings, and that was a great cheer to my spirits. It was at a public-house in Fashion-street. I went into the tap-room and asked the gentlemen if they would wish to hear a recitation from Shakspeare, and they said, 'Proceed'. The first part I gave them was from 'Richard III': 'Now is the winter of our discontent'; and then they clapped me and made me do it over again. Then I performed Hamlet's 'Soliloquy on the

Immortality of the Soul,' and they threw down two shillings in coppers, and one gentleman gave me sixpence.

I've continued giving recitations from Shakespeare and selections from the poets ever since, and done very well, until I became ill with a cold, which made my voice bad, so that I was unable to speak. I've been ill now a fortnight, and I went out last night for the first time, along with another young fellow who recites, and we got one and sixpence between us in the 'Gipsy's Revenge'. We went to a public-house where they were having 'a lead', that is a collection for a friend who is ill, and the company throw down what they can for a subscription, and they have in a fiddle and make it social. But it was not a good 'lead', and poorly attended, so we did not make much out of the company.

When I go out to recite, I generally go with another boy, and we take parts. The pieces that draw best with the public are, 'The Gipsy's Revenge', 'The Gold Digger's Revenge', 'The Miser', 'The Robber', 'The Felon', and 'The Highwayman'. We take parts in these, and he always performs the villain, and I take the noble characters. He always dies, because he can do a splendid back-fall, and he looks so wicked when he's got the moustaches on. I generally draws the company by giving two or three recitations, and then we perform a piece; and whilst he goes round with the hat, I recite again. My favourite recitations are, 'Othello's Apology', beginning with 'Most potent, grave, and reverend Signiors', and those from Hamlet, Richard III, and Macbeth. Of the recitations I think the people prefer that from Othello, for the ladies have often asked me to give them that from Othello (they like to hear about Desdemona), but the gentlemen ask for that from Hamlet, 'To be, or not to be?'

My principal place for giving performances is the Commercial-road, near Limehouse, but the most theatrically inclined neighbourhood is the Walworth-road. The most money I ever took at one time in the streets was four shillings in the Walworth-road.

The best receipts I ever had was got in a public-house near Brick-lane, for I took twelve shillings, and I was alone. There was a 'lead' up there for a friend, and I knew of it, and I had my hair curled and got myself decently habited, I was there for about three or four hours, and in the intervals between the dances I used to recite. There were girls there, and they took my part, though they made me drink so much I was nearly tipsy.

The only theatrical costume I put on is moustachios, and I take a stick to use as a sword. I put myself into attitudes, and look as fierce as I can. When first the people came to hear me they laughed, and then they became quiet; and sometimes you could hear a pin drop.

When I am at work regularly – that's when I am in voice and will – I make about ten shillings a-week, if there's not much rain. If it's wet, people don't go to the public-houses, and they are my best paying audiences. The least I have ever taken in a week is about 6s.

There isn't many going about London reciting. It is a very rare class to be found; I only know about four who live that way, and I have heard of the others from hearsay – not that I have seen them myself.[50]

Mayhew got a glimpse of different literary tastes from a conversation with a boy in a workhouse.

I am now seventeen. My father was a cotton-spinner in Manchester, but has been dead ten years; and soon after that my mother went into the workhouse, leaving me with an aunt; and I had work in a cotton factory. As young as I was, I earned two shillings and twopence a-week at first. I can read well, and can write a little. I worked at the factory two years, and was then earning seven shillings a-week. I then ran away, for I had always a roving mind; but I should have stayed if my master hadn't knocked me about so. I thought I should make my fortune in London – I'd heard it was such a grand place. I had read in novels and romances – halfpenny and penny books – about such things, but I've met with nothing of the kind. I started without money, and begged my way from Manchester to London, saying I was going up to look for work. I wanted to see the place more than anything else. I suffered very much on the road, having to be out all night often; and the nights were cold, though it was summer. When I got to London all my hopes were blighted. I could get no further. I never tried for work in London, for I believe there are no cotton factories in it; besides, I wanted to see life. I begged, and slept in the unions. I got acquainted with plenty of boys like myself. We met at the casual wards, both in London and the country. I have now been five years at this life. We were merry enough in the wards, we boys, singing and telling stories. Songs such as 'Paul Jones' was liked, while some sung very blackguard songs; but I never got hold of such songs, though I have sold lots of songs in Essex. Some told long stories, very interesting; some were not fit to be heard; but they made one laugh sometimes. I've read 'Jack Sheppard' through, in three volumes; and I used to tell stories out of that sometimes. We all told in our turns. We generally began, 'Once upon a time, and a very good time it was, though it was neither in your time, nor my time, nor nobody else's time.' The best man in the story is always called Jack.

At my request, this youth told me a long story, and told it very readily, as if by rote. I give it for its peculiarity, as it is extravagant enough, without humour.

A farmer hired Jack, and instructed him over-night. Jack was to do what he was required, or lose his head. 'Now, Jack,' said the farmer, [I give the conclusion in the boy's words,] 'what's my name?' 'Master, to be sure,' says Jack. 'No,' said he, 'you must call me Tom Per Cent.' He showed his bed next, and asked, 'What's this, Jack?' 'Why, the bed,' said Jack. 'No, you must call that, He's of Degree.' And so he bid Jack call his leather breeches 'forty cracks'; the cat, 'white-faced Simeon'; the fire, 'hot coleman'; the pump, the 'resurrection'; and the haystack, the 'little cock-a-mountain'. Jack was to remember these names or lose his head. At night the cat got under the grate, and burned herself, and a hot cinder struck her fur, and she ran under the haystack and set it on fire. Jack ran up-stairs to his master, and said:

Tom Per Cent, arise out of he's of degree,
Put on your forty cracks, come down and see;
For the little white-faced Simeon
Has run away with hot coleman
Under the little cock-a-mountain,
And without the aid of the resurrection
We shall be damned and burnt to death.

So Jack remembered his lesson, and saved his head. That's the end. Blackguard stories were often told about women. There was plenty told, too, about Dick Turpin, Sixteenstring Jack, Oxford Blue, and such as them; as well as about Jack Sheppard; about Bamfylde Moore Carew, too, and his disguises.[51]

Chapter Nine: Gathering Facts

The interviews in London Labour and the London Poor *make up such a large proportion of the writings that it's easy to forget that Mayhew's initial intention was as much to gather facts and data about the poor working people of London as it was to record long personal interviews with them. But there are many lists of facts and tables of data in the work, from the famous example of the amount of horse manure dropped on the streets of London in a year, (118,043.25 tons) to the annual turnover of London's street-sellers of stationery. Although Mayhew sometimes relied on material published by others his writing also shows evidence of his own careful, even obsessive, data-gathering and calculations.*

The diet of the poor

In the first place [...] it appears that in the matter of fish, herrings constitute the chief article of consumption – no less than 210,000,000 lbs. weight of this fish in a 'fresh' state, and 60,000,000 lbs. in a 'dried' state, being annually eaten by the humbler classes of the metropolis and the suburbs. Of sprats there are 3,000,000 lbs. weight consumed – and these, with the addition of plaice, are the staple comestibles at the dinners and suppers of the ichthyóphagous part of the labouring population of London. One of the reasons for this is doubtless the extraordinary cheapness of these kinds of fish. The sprats are sold at a penny per pound; the herrings at the same rate; and the plaice at a fraction less, perhaps; whereas a pound of butcher's meat, even 'pieces', or the 'block ornaments', as they are sometimes called, cannot be got for less than twopence-halfpenny or threepence. But the relative cheapness of these two kinds of food can only be tested by the proportionate quantity of nutrition in each. According to Liebig, butcher's meat contains twenty-six per cent of solid matter, and seventy-four per cent of water; whereas, according to Brande, fish consists of twenty parts of solid matter, and eighty parts water in every 100. Hence it would appear that butcher's meat is five per cent more nutritive than fish – or, in other words, that if the two were equally cheap, the prices, according to the quantity of nutrition in each, should be for fish one penny per pound, and butcher's meat not five farthings; so that even at twopence-halfpenny the pound, meat is more than twice as dear an article of diet as fish.

But it is not only on account of their cheapness that herrings and sprats are consumed in such vast quantities by the labouring people of London. Salmon, eels, herrings, pilchards, and sprats, Dr Pereira tells us, abound in oil; and oleaginous food, according to Leibig, is an 'element of respiration', consisting of nearly eighty per cent charcoal, which burns away in the lungs, and so contributes to the warmth of the system. Fat, indeed, may be said to act as fuel to the vital fire; and we now know, from observations made upon the average daily consumption of food by twenty-eight soldiers of the Grand Duke of Hesse Darmstadt, in barracks, for a month – which is the same as 840 men for one day – that an adult taking moderate exercise consumes, in the act of respiration, very nearly a pound of charcoal every day, which of course must be supplied in his food. 'But persons who take much exercise, or labour hard,' says Dr Pereira, 'require more frequent and copious meals than the indolent or sedentary. In the active man the number of respirations is greater than in the inactive, and therefore a more frequent supply of food is required to furnish the increased quantity of carbon and hydrogen to be consumed in the lungs.' 'A bird deprived of food,' says Liebig, 'dies on the third day; while a serpent, with its sluggish respiration, can live without food three months, or longer.'

Captain Parry, in his account of one of the Polar expeditions (1827), states, that both himself and Mr Beverley, the surgeon, were of opinion, that, in order to maintain the strength of the men during their harassing journey across the ice, living constantly in the open air, and exposed to the wet and cold for twelve hours a day, an addition was requisite of at least one third to the quantity of provisions daily issued. So, in the gaol dietaries, the allowance to prisoners sentenced to hard labour for three months is one-third more than the scale for those sentenced to hard labour for three days – the former having 254 ounces, and the latter only 168 ounces of solid food served out to them every week.

But the hard-working poor not only require more food than the non-working rich, but it is mainly because the rich are better fed that they are more lethargic than the poor; for the greater the supply of nutriment to the body, the more inactive does the system become. From experiments made a few years ago at the Zoological Gardens, it was found, that, by feeding the animals twice, instead of once, in the twenty-four-hours, their habits, as regards exercise, were altered – a fact which readily explains how the fat and overfed are always the least energetic; fat being at once the cause and consequence of inaction. It is well to hear an obese citizen tell a hollow-cheeked man, who begs a penny of him, 'to go and work – a lazy scoundrel'; but physiology assures us that the fat tradesman is naturally the laziest of the two. In a word, he is fat because he is lazy, and lazy because he is fat.

The industrious poor, however, not only require more food than the indolent rich, but, getting less, they become more susceptible of cold, and, therefore, more eager for all that tends to promote warmth. I have often had occasion to remark the sacrifices that the ill-fed will make to have 'a bit of fire'. 'He who is well fed,' observes Sir John Ross, 'resists cold better than the man who is stinted, while starvation from cold follows but too soon a starvation in food. This doubtlessly explains in a great measure the resisting powers of the natives of frozen climates, their consumption of food being enormous, and often incredible.' Captain Cochrane, in his 'Journey through Russia and Siberian Tartary', tells us that he has repeatedly seen a Yakut or Tongouse devour forty pounds of meat in a day; and one of the Yakuti he speaks of as having consumed, in twenty-four hours, 'the hind-quarter of a large ox, twenty pounds of fat, and a proportionate quantity of melted butter for his drink'. Much less heat is evolved, physiologists tell us, where there is a deficiency of food. 'During the whole of our march,' says Sir John Franklin, 'we experienced that no quantity of clothing could keep us warm while we fasted; but, on those occasions on which we were enabled to go to bed with full stomachs, we passed the night in a warm and comfortable manner.' Hence, it is evident, that in summer a smaller quantity of food suffices to keep up the temperature of the body. I know of no experiments to show the different proportions of aliment required at different seasons of the year. In winter, however, when a greater supply is certainly needed, the labouring man, unfortunately, has less means of obtaining it – nearly all trades slacken as the cold weather comes on, and some, as brick-making, market-gardening, building, &c., then almost entirely cease – so that, were it not for the cheapness of fish, and, moreover, the oleaginous quality of those kinds which are most plentiful in the winter time, the metropolitan poor would be very likely to suffer that 'starvation from cold which', in the words of Sir John Ross, 'follows but too soon a starvation in food". Hence we can readily understand the remark of the enthusiastic street-seller: 'Sprats *is* a blessing to the poor.'

The returns as to the other articles of food sold in the streets are equally curious. The £1,500,000 spent yearly in fish, and the comparatively small amount expended on vegetables, viz.,

£290,000, is a circumstance which seems to show that the labouring population of London have a greater relish for animal than vegetable diet. 'It is quite certain,' says Dr. Carpenter, 'that the most perfect physical development and the greatest intellectual vigour are to be found among those races in which a mixed diet of animal and vegetable food is the prevalent habit.' And yet, in apparent contradiction to the proposition asserted with so much confidence by Dr Carpenter, we have the following curious fact cited by Mr Jacob Bentley:

It is, indeed, a fact worthy of remark, and one that seems never to have been noticed, that throughout the whole animal creation, in every country and clime of the earth the most useful animals cost nature the least waste to sustain them with food. For instance, all animals that work, live on vegetable or fruit food; and no animal that eats flesh, works. The all-powerful elephant, and the patient, untiring camel in the torrid zone; the horse, the ox, or the donkey in the temperate, and the reindeer in the frigid zone; obtain all their muscular power for enduring labour, from Nature's simplest productions – the vegetable kingdom.

But all the flesh-eating animals, keep the rest of the animated creation in constant dread of them. They seldom eat vegetable food till some other animal has eaten it first, and made it into flesh. Their only use seems to be, to destroy life; their own flesh is unfit for other animals to eat, having been itself made out of flesh, and is most foul and offensive. Great strength, fleetness of foot, usefulness, cleanliness and docility, are then always characteristic of vegetable eating animals, while all the world dreads flesheaters.

Of vegetables we have seen that the greatest quantity consumed by the poor consists of potatoes, of which 60,500,000 lbs. are annually sold in the streets; but ten pounds of potatoes are only equal in nutritive power to one pound of butcher's meat, which contains one-fifth more solid food than fish – so that a pound of fish may be said to equal eight pounds of potatoes, and thus the 60,000,000 lbs. of vegetable is dietetically equivalent to nearly 7,000,000 lbs. of fish diet. The cost of the potatoes, at five pounds for 2*d.*, is, as we have seen, £100,000; whereas the cost of the same amount of nutritive matter in the form of fish, at a penny per pound, would have been only £30,000, or upwards of two-thirds less. The vegetable of which there is the next greatest street sale is onions, upon which £90,000 are annually expended. This has been before accounted for, by saying, that a piece of bread and an onion are to the English labourer what bread and grapes are to the Frenchman – oftentimes a meal. The relish for onions by the poorer classes is not difficult to explain. Onions are strongly stimulating substances, and they owe their peculiar odour and flavour, as well as their pungent and stimulating qualities, to an acrid volatile oil which contains sulphur. This oil becomes absorbed, quickens the circulation, and occasions thirst. The same result takes place with the oil of fish. It not only proves a stimulant to the general system, but we are told that the thirst and uneasy feeling at the stomach, frequently experienced after the use of the richer species of fish, have led to the employment of spirit to this kind of food. Hence, says Dr Pereira, the vulgar proverb, 'Brandy is Latin for Fish'. Moreover, the two classes of food are similar in their comparative indigestibility, for the uneducated palates of the poor not only require a more pungent kind of diet, but their stronger stomachs need something that will resist the action of the gastric juice for a considerable time. Hence their love of shellfish.

The small quantity of fruit, too, sold to the poor is a further proof of what is here stated. The amount of the street sale of this luxury is no criterion as to the quantity purchased by the

London labourers; for according to all accounts the fruit-buyers in the streets consist mostly of clerks, shopmen, small tradesmen, and the children of mechanics or the lower grade of middle-class people. Those who may be said strictly to belong to the poor – viz. those whose incomes are barely sufficient for their support – seldom purchase fruit. In the first place they have no money to spend on such a mere toothsome extravagance; and, secondly, they require a stronger and more stimulating, and 'staying' kind of food. The delights of the palate, we should remember, are studied only when the cravings of the stomach are satisfied, so that those who have strong stomachs have necessarily dull palates, and, therefore, prefer something that 'bites in the mouth' – to use the words of one of my informants – like gin, onions, sprats, or pickled whelks. What the poor term 'relishes' are very different things from what the rich style the 'delicacies of the season'.

I have no means of ascertaining the average number of ounces of solid food consumed by the poorer class of the metropolis. The *whole* of the fish, fruit, and vegetables, sold to the London costermongers, is not disposed of in the London streets – many of the street-sellers going, as we have seen, country excursions with their goods. According to the result of the Government Commissioners of Inquiry, the labourers in the country are unable to procure for themselves and families an average allowance of more than 122 ounces of solid food – principally bread – every week; hence it has been justly said we may infer that the man consumes, as his share, 140 ounces (134 bread and 6 meat). The gaol dietaries allow 254 ounces, or nearly twice as much to all prisoners, who undergo continuous hard labour. In the construction of these dietaries Sir James Graham – the then Secretary of State – says, in his 'Letter to the Chairman of Quarter Sessions' (27th January 1843), 'I have consulted not only the Prison Inspectors, but medical men of the greatest eminence possessing the advantage of long experience.' They are proposed, he adds, 'as the *minimum* amount which can be safely afforded to prisoners without the risk of inflicting a punishment not contemplated by law and which it is unjust and cruel to inflict; namely, loss of health and strength through the inadequacy of the food supplied'. Hence it appears not that the thief gets too much, but the honest working man too little – or, in other words, that the labourer of this country is able to procure, by his industry, only half the quantity of food that is considered by 'medical men of the greatest eminence' to be 'the *minimum* amount' that can be *safely* afforded for the support of the criminals – a fact which it would be out of place to comment upon here.[52]

The annual takings of street-sellers of stationery, literature and the fine arts

Street-sellers of stationery

There are 120 vendors of stationery, who sell altogether during the year, 224,640 quires of writing paper at threepence per quire; 149,760 doz. envelopes, at a penny halfpenny per doz.; 37,440 doz. pens, at threepence per doz.; 24,960 bottles of ink, at a penny each; 112,320 black lead pencils, at a penny each; 24,960 pennyworths of wafers, and 49,920 sticks of sealing-wax, at a halfpenny per stick; amounting altogether to £4,992.

Street-sellers of pocket-books and diaries

During the year 1,440 pocket-books, at sixpence each, and 960 diaries, at sixpence each, are sold in the streets by twenty vendors; amounting to £60.

Street-sellers of almanacks and memorandum-books

There are sold during the year, in the streets of London, 280,800 memorandum-books, at a penny each, and 4,800 almanacks at a penny each, among fifty vendors, altogether amounting to £1,190.

Street-sellers of account-books

There are now twelve itinerants vending account-books in various parts of the metropolis, each of whom sells daily, upon an average, four account-books, at a shilling and ninepence each; the number sold during the year is therefore 14,976, and the sum expended thereon amounts to £1,310.

Street-sellers of 'gelatine', 'engraved', and 'playing-cards'

There are twenty street-sellers vending gelatine and engraved cards during the day, and thirty selling playing-cards (for fourteen days) at night. These vendors get rid of, among them, in the course of the year, 43,200 gelatine, and 14,400 engraved cards, at a penny each, and 3,360 packs of playing-cards, at threepence per pack; so that the money spent in the streets on the sale of engraved, gelatine, and playing-cards, during the year, amounts to £282.

Street-seller of stenographic cards

There is only one individual 'working' stenographic cards in the streets of London, and the number he sells in the course of the year is 7,448 cards, at a penny each, amounting to £31 4s.

Street-sellers of long songs

I am assured, that if twenty persons were selling long songs in the street last summer (during a period of twelve weeks), it was 'the outside'; as long songs are now 'for fairs and races, and country work'. Calculating that each cleared nine shillings in a week, and to clear that took fifteen shillings, we find there is expended in long songs in the streets annually £180.

Street-sellers of wall songs ('pinners-up')

On fine summer days, the wall song-sellers (of whom there are thirty) take two shillings on an average. On short wintry days they may not take half so much, and on very foggy or rainy days they take nothing at all. Reckoning that each wall song-man now takes ten shillings and sixpence weekly (seven shillings being the profit), we find there is expended yearly in London streets, in the ballads of the pinners-up £810.

Street-sellers of Ballads ('chaunters')

There are now 200 chaunters, who also sell the ballads they sing; the average takings of each are three shillings per day; altogether amounting to £4,680.

Street-sellers of executions, &c. ('running patterers')

Some represent their average weekly earnings at twelve shillings and sixpence the year through; some at ten shillings and sixpence; and others at less than half of twelve shillings and sixpence. Reckoning, however, that only nine shillings weekly is an average profit per individual, and that fourteen shillings be taken to realise that profit, we find there is expended yearly, on executions, fires, deaths, &c., in London £3,276.

Street-sellers of dialogues, litanies, &c. (standing patterers)

If twenty standing patterers clear ten shillings weekly, each, the year through, and take fifteen shillings weekly, we find there is yearly expended in the standing patter of London streets £780.

Street-sellers of 'cocks' (elopements, love letters, &c.)

There are now eight men who sell nothing but 'cocks', each of whom dispose daily of six dozen copies at a halfpenny per copy, or altogether, during the year, 179,712 copies, amounting to £374 8s.

Street-sellers of conundrums – 'nuts to crack', &c.

From the best information I could acquire, it appears that fifteen men may be computed as working conundrums for two months throughout the twelve, and clearing ten shillings and sixpence weekly, per individual. The cost of the 'nuts to crack' (when new) is fivepence a dozen to the seller; but old 'nuts' often answer the purpose of the street-seller, and may be had for about half the price; the cost of the 'nut-crackers' is two shillings to two shillings and sixpence. It may be calculated, then, that to realize the ten shillings and sixpence above-mentioned fifteen shillings must be taken. This shows the street expenditure in 'nuts to crack' and 'nut-crackers' to be yearly £90.

Street-sellers of exhibition papers, magical delusions, &c.

This trade is carried on only for a short time in the winter, as regards the magical portion; and I am informed that, including the 'comic exhibitions', it extends to about half of the sum taken for conundrums; or to about £45.

Street-sellers of secret papers

Supposing that six men last year each cleared six shillings weekly, we find expended yearly in the streets on this rubbish £93.

Street-sellers of play-bills and books

Taking the profits at three shillings a week, at cent. per cent. on the outlay, and reckoning 200 sellers, including those at the saloons, concert-rooms, &c., there is expended yearly on the sale of play-bills purchased in the streets of London £3,120

Street-sellers of back numbers

There are now forty vendors in the streets of London, each selling upon an average three-dozen copies daily, at a halfpenny each, or during the year 336,960 odd numbers. Hence, the sum expended annually in the streets for back numbers of periodicals amounts to upwards of £700.

Street-sellers of waste-paper at Billingsgate

There are four individuals selling waste-paper at Billingsgate, one of whom informed me that from 70 to 100 pounds weight of 'waste' – about three-fourths being newspapers – is supplied to Billingsgate market and its visitants. The average price is not less than twopence halfpenny a pound, or from that to threepence. A single paper is a penny. Reckoning that 85 pounds of waste-paper are sold a day, at twopence halfpenny per pound, we find that the annual expenditure in waste-paper at Billingsgate is upwards of £275.

Street-sellers of tracts and pamphlets

From the information I obtained from one of this class of street-sellers, I find there are forty individuals gaining a livelihood in selling tracts and pamphlets in the streets, full one half are men of colour, the other half consists of old and infirm men, and young boys, the average takings of each is about a shilling a day, the year through; the annual street expenditure in the sale of tracts and pamphlets is thus upwards of £620.

Street-sellers of newspapers (second edition)

There are twenty who are engaged in the street sale of newspapers, second edition, each of whom take weekly (for a period of six weeks in the year) one pound five shillings.; so that, adopting the calculation of my informant, and giving a profit of 150 per cent., the yearly expenditure in the streets, in second editions, amounts to £150.

Street-sellers of newspapers, &c., at steam-boat piers

I am informed that the average earnings of these traders, altogether, may be taken at fifteen shillings weekly; calculating that twelve carry on the trade the year through, we find that (assuming each man to sell at thirty-three per cent. profit – though in the case of old works it will be often cent. per cent.), the sum expended annually in steam-boat papers is upwards of £1,500.

Street-sellers of books (by auction)

There are at present only two street-sellers of books by auction in London, whose clear weekly earnings are ten shillings and sixpence each. Calculating their profits at £250 per cent., their weekly receipts will amount to thirty-five shillings each per week; giving a yearly expenditure of £91.

Street-sellers of books on stalls and barrows

The number of book-stalls and barrows in the streets of the metropolis is seventy. The proprietors of these sell weekly upon an average forty-two volumes each. The number of volumes annually sold in the streets is thus 1,375,920, and reckoning each volume sold to average ninepence, we find that the yearly expenditure in the sale of books in the street amounts to £5,733.

Street-sellers of guide-books

The street-sellers of guide-books to public places of amusement, are sixteen in number, the profit of each is four shillings weekly, at twenty-five per cent., hence the takings must be twenty shillings; thus making the annual expenditure in the street-sale of such books amount to £832.

Street-sale of song-books and children's books

There are thirty street-sellers who vend children's books and song-books, and dispose of, among them, two dozen each daily, or during the year 224,640 books, at a penny each; hence the sum yearly expended in the street-sale of children's books and song-books is £936.

Street-sellers of pictures in frames

If we calculate forty persons selling pictures in frames, and each taking 10s. weekly; we find the annual amount spent in the streets in the sale of these articles is £1,040.

Street-sellers of prints and engravings in umbrellas

The street-sale of prints and engravings in umbrellas lasts only twelve weeks. There are thirty individuals who gain a livelihood in the sale of these articles during that period. The average takings of each seller is twelve shillings weekly; so that the annual street-expenditure upon prints and engravings is £216.

Street-sellers of manuscript music

There are only four sellers of manuscript music in the streets, who take on an average four shillings each weekly; hence we find the annual expenditure in this article amounts in round numbers to £40.

Total Sum Expended Yearly in the Streets on Stationery, Literature, and the Fine Arts:
£33,446 12s.[53]

It might seem excessive to go into the kind of detail that Mayhew does in his data-trawls through every aspect of London street life. But where else could one learn, as in the next extract, of the detailed contents of a 'swag shop'? This sold 'every variety of article, apart from what is eatable, drinkable, or wearable' and offered cheap, often shoddily-made, household goods at prices low enough for poor working people to afford:

On saturday afternoons pale-looking men may be seen carrying a few chairs, or bending under the weight of a cheffonier or a chest of drawers, in Tottenham-court Road, and thoroughfares of a similar character in all parts. These are 'small masters', who make or (as one man said to me, 'No, sir, I don't make these drawers, I put them together, it can't be called making; it's not workmanship') who 'put together' in the hastiest manner, and in any way not positively offensive to the eye, articles of household furniture. The 'slaughterers' who supply all the goods required for the furniture of a house, buy at 'starvation prices' (the common term), the artificer being often kept waiting for hours, and treated with every indignity. One East-end 'slaughterer' (as I ascertained in a former inquiry) used habitually to tell that he prayed for wet Saturday afternoons, because it put £20 extra into his pocket! This was owing to the damage sustained in the appearance of any painted, varnished, or polished article, by exposure to the weather; or if it had been protected from the weather, by the unwillingness of the small master to carry it to another slaughter-house in the rain. Under such circumstances – and under most of the circumstances of this unhappy trade – the poor workman is at the mercy of the slaughterer.

I describe this matter more fully than I might have deemed necessary, had I not found that both the 'small masters' spoken of – for I called upon some of them again – and the street-sellers, very frequently confounded the 'swag-shop' and the 'slaughter-house'. The distinction I hold to be this: the slaughterer buys as a rule, with hardly an exception, the furniture, or whatever it may be, made for the express purpose of being offered to him on speculation of sale. The swag shop-keeper *orders* his goods as a rule, and buys, as an exception, in the manner in which the slaughterer buys ordinarily. The slaughterer sells by retail; the swag-shop keeper only by wholesale.

Most of the articles, of the class of which I now treat, are 'Brummagem made'. An experienced tradesman said to me: 'All these low-priced metal things, fancy goods and all, which you see about, are made in Birmingham; in nineteen cases out of twenty at the least. They may be marked London, or Sheffield, or Paris, or any place – you can have them marked North Pole if you will – but they're genuine Birmingham. The carriage is lower from Birmingham than from Sheffield – that's one thing.'

The majority of the swag-shop proprietors are Jews. The wares which they supply to the cheap shops, the cheap John's, and the street-sellers, in town and country, consist of every variety of article, apart from what is eatable, drinkable, or wearable, in which the trade class I have specified can deal. As regards what is wearable, indeed, such things as braces, garters, &c., form a portion of the stock of the swag-shop.

In one street (a thoroughfare at the east-end of London) are twenty-three of these establishments. In the windows there is little attempt at display; the design aimed at seems to be rather to *crowd* the window – as if to show the amplitude of the stores within, 'the wonderful resources of this most extensive and universal establishment' – than to tempt purchasers by exhibiting tastefully what may have been tastefully executed by the artificer, or what it is desired should be held to be so executed.

In one of these windows the daylight is almost precluded from the interior by what may be called a perfect wall of 'pots'. A street-seller who accompanied me called them merely 'pots' (the trade term), but they were all pot ornaments. Among them were great store of shepherdesses, of greyhounds of a gamboge colour, of what I heard called 'figures' (allegorical nymphs with and without birds or wreaths in their hands), very tall-looking Shakespeares (I did not see one of these windows without its Shakespeare, a sitting figure), and some 'pots' which seem to be either shepherds or musicians; from what I could learn, at the pleasure of the seller, the buyer, or the inquirer. The shepherd, or musician is usually seated under a tree; he wears a light blue coat, and yellow breeches, and his limbs, more than his body, are remarkable for their bulk; to call them merely fat does not sufficiently express their character, and in some 'pots', they are as short and stumpy as they are bulky. On my asking if the dogs were intended for Italian greyhounds, I was told, 'No, they are German.' I alluded however to the species of the animal represented; my informant to the place of manufacture, for the pots were chiefly German. A number of mugs however, with the Crystal Palace very well depicted upon them, were unmistakably English. In another window of the same establishment was a conglomeration of pincushions, shaving-brushes, letter-stamps (all in bone), cribbage-boards and boxes (including a pack of cards), necklaces, and strings of beads.

The window of a neighbouring swag-shop presented, in the like crowding, and in greater confusion, an array of brooches (some in coloured glass to imitate rubies, topazes, &c., some containing portraits, deeply coloured, in purple attire, and red cheeks, and some being very large cameos), time-pieces (with and without glasses), French toys with moveable figures, telescopes, American clocks, musical boxes, shirt-studs, backgammon-boards, tea-trays (one with a nondescript bird of most gorgeous green plumage forming a sort of centrepiece), razor-strops, writing-desks, sailors' knives, hair-brushes, and tobacco-boxes.

Another window presented even a more 'miscellaneous assortment'; dirks (apparently not very formidable weapons), a mess of steel pens, in brown-paper packages and cases, and of black-lead pencils, pipe-heads, cigar-cases, snuff-boxes, razors, shaving-brushes, letter-stamps, metal tea-pots, metal tea-spoons, glass globes with artificial flowers and leaves within the glass (an improvement one man thought on the old ornament of a reel in a bottle), Peel medals, Exhibition medals, roulette-boxes, scent bottles, quill pens with artificial flowers in the feathery part, fans, side-combs, glass pen-holders, and pot figures (caricatures) of Louis Philippe, carrying a very red umbrella, Marshal Haynau, with some instrument of torture in his hand, while over all boomed a huge English seaman, in yellow waistcoat and with a brick-coloured face.

Sometimes the furniture of a swag-shop window is less plentiful, but quite as heterogenous. In one were only American clocks, French toys (large), opera-glasses, knives and forks, and powder-flasks.

In some windows the predominant character is jewellery. Ear-drops (generally gilt), rings of all kinds, brooches of every size and shade of coloured glass, shawl-pins, shirt-studs, necklaces, bead purses, small paintings of the Crystal-palace, in 'burnished "gold" frames', watch-guards, watch-seals (each with three impressions or mottoes), watch-chains and keys, 'silver' tooth-picks, medals, and snuff-boxes. It might be expected that the jewellery shops would present the most imposing display of any; they are, on the contrary, among the dingiest, as if it were not worth the trouble to put clean things in the window, but merely what sufficed to characterise the nature of the trade carried on.

Of the twenty-three swag-shops in question, five were confined to the trade in all the branches of stationery. Of these I saw one, the large window of which was perfectly packed from bottom to top with note-paper, account and copy-books, steel-pens, pencils, sealing-wax, enamelled wafers (in boxes), ink-stands, &c.

Of the other shops, two had cases of watches, with no attempt at display, or even arrangement. 'Poor things,' I was told by a person familiar with the trade in them, 'fit only to offer to countrymen when they've been drinking at a fair, and think themselves clever.'

I have so far described the exterior of these street-dealers' bazaars, the swag-shops, in what may be called their headquarters. Upon entering some of these places of business, spacious rooms are seen to extend behind the shop or warehouse which opens to the street. Some are almost blocked up with what appears a litter of packing-cases, packages, and bales – but which are no doubt ordered systematically enough – while the shelves are crammed with goods in brown paper, or in cases or boxes. This uniformity of package, so to speak, has the effect of destroying the true character of these swag store-rooms; for they present the appearance of only three or four different kinds of merchandise being deposited on a range of shelves, when, perhaps, there are a hundred. In some of these swag-shops it appears certain, both from what fell under my own observation, and from what I learned through my inquiries of persons long familiar with such places, that the 'litter' I have spoken of is disposed so as to present the appearance of an affluence of goods without the reality of possession.

In no warehouses (properly 'swag', or wholesale traders) is there any arranged display of the wares vended. 'Ve don't vant people here,' one street-seller had often heard a swag-shopkeeper say, 'as looks about them, and says, "Ow purty! – Vot nice things!" Ve vants to sell, and not to show. Ve is all for bisness, and be damned.' All of these places which I saw were dark, more or less so, in the interior, as if a customer's inspection were uncared for.

Some of the swag-shop people present cards, or 'circulars with prices', to their street and other customers, calling attention to the variety of their wares. These circulars are not given without inquiry, as if it were felt that one must not be wasted. On one I find the following enumeration:

Shopkeepers and Dealers supplied with the following Articles:

Clocks – American, French, German, and English eight-day dials.
Watches – gold and silver.
Musical boxes – two, four, six, and eight airs.
Watch-glasses – common flint, geneva, and lunettes.
Main-Springs – blue and straw-colour, English and Geneva.
Watch materials – of every description.
Jewellery – a general assortment.
Spectacles – gold, silver, steel, horn, and metal frames, concave, convex, coloured, and smoked eyes.
Telescopes – one, two, and three draws.
Mathematical Instruments.
Combs – side, dressing, curl, pocket, ivory, small-tooth, &c.
Musical instruments – violins, violincellos, bows, &c., flutes, clarionets, trombones, ophoclides, cornopeans, French-horns, post-horns, trumpets, and passes, violin tailboards, pegs, and bridges.
Accordions – French and German of every size and style.

It must not be thought that swag-shops are mainly repositories of 'fancy' articles, for such is not the case. I have described only the 'windows' and outward appearances of these places – the interior being little demonstrative of the business; but the bulkier and more useful articles of swag traffic cannot be exposed in a window…

The swag-shops (of which I state the numbers in a parenthesis) are in Houndsditch (their principal locality) (23), Minories (4), Whitechapel (2), Ratcliffe-highway (20), Shoreditch (1), Long-lane, Smithfield (4), Fleet-lane (2), Holywell-street, Strand (1), Tothill-street (4), Compton-street, Soho (1), Hatton-garden (2), Clerkenwell (10), Kent-street, Borough (8), New-cut (6), Black-man-street (2), Tooley-street (3), London-road (3), Borough-road (1), Waterloo-road (4) – in all 101; but a person who had been upwards of twenty years a frequenter of these places counted up fifty others, many of them in obscure courts and alleys near Houndsditch, Ratcliffe Highway, &c., &c. These 'outsiders' are generally of a smaller class than those I have described; 'And I can tell you, sir,' the same man said, 'some of them – ay, and some of the big ones, too – are real swag-shops still – partly so, that is; you understand me, sir.' The word 'swag', I should inform my polite readers, means in slang language, 'plunder'.[54]

Notes

1. John D. Rosenberg, introduction to *London Labour and the London Poor,* Vol. 1, Dover Publications, 1968, p. vii

2. Karel Williams, *From Pauperism to Poverty*, London: Routledge & Kegan Paul, 1981, p. 266.

3. Henry Mayhew and John Binney, *The Criminal Prisons of London*, Griffin, Bohn and Company, 1862, p. iv

4. Henry Mayhew, *Voices of Victorian London, In Sickness and in Health*, Hesperus Press, 2011

5. *Punch*, 9 March 1850, p. 93

6. Anne Humphreys, introduction to *Voices of the Poor* by Henry Mayhew, Frank Cass, 1971, p. xiii

7. 3–312

8. 3–302

9. M-0-1-267

10. M-6-1-324

11. M-0-1-438

12. M-1-1-202

13. M-3-1-358

14. M-4-1-071*

15. M-3-1-362*

16. 1-155

17. 2-451

18. M-6-1-452*

19. M-7-1-359*

20. M-0-1-091-2

21. M-0-1-326*

22. M-0-1-401*

23. M-1-1-410*

24. M-4-1-279*

25. M-3-1-379*

26. M-0-1-061

27. M-0-1-367

28. M-0-1-032a

29. M-0-1-032-2

30. M-0-1-061

31. M-0-1-077

32. M-4-1-068*

33. M-4-1-068*

34. M-0-1-234*

35. M-0-1-363

36. M-0-1-445*
37. M-0-1-377*
38. M-2-1-414*
39. M-0-1-351*
40. M-0-3-206*
41. 1-109
42. 2-503
43. 2-64
44. 3-306
45. 3-251
46. Morning Chronicle, LETTER IV *Tuesday, October 30, 1849*
47. *Comic Almanac* 1851, pp. 347–50
48. 1-292
49. 1-228
50. M-0-3-151
51. M-17-3-390
52. 1-118
53. 1-306
54. 1-333

Biographical Note

Henry Mayhew was an English journalist, author and social reformer. Born in London in 1812, he was educated at Westminster School and served as a midshipman in the East India Company. On his return to England he briefly underwent legal training before taking up freelance writing. In 1835 he fled to Paris to escape his creditors.

In 1841 Mayhew co-founded the satirical magazine *Punch* and from 1842 began contributing to the *Illustrated London News*, becoming financially secure enough to settle his debts and return to England.

In 1849, after a cholera epidemic killed over 10,000 Londoners, Mayhew began observing and conducting interviews with the poor working people of London, initially for a series of articles in the *London Chronicle*. These articles went into meticulous detail concerning the lives, living conditions and occupations of the working classes, as well as the daily struggles of itinerants and beggars. These articles were collected and published in book form in 1851, in the three-volume *London Labour and the London Poor*. A fourth volume, published with the 1861 edition, focused on petty criminals, prostitutes and vagrants. Mayhew's work exerted considerable influence over radicals and socialists, but also over Charles Dickens, whose novels featured characters inspired by some of Mayhew's subjects.

Henry Mayhew died in 1887 and is buried in Kensal Green.

Karl Sabbagh is a British-Palestinian writer and television producer. He lives in Warwickshire.

HESPERUS PRESS

Hesperus Press is committed to bringing near what is far – far both in space and time. Works written by the greatest authors, and unjustly neglected or simply little known in the English-speaking world, are made accessible through new translations and a completely fresh editorial approach. Through these classic works, the reader is introduced to the greatest writers from all times and all cultures.

For more information on Hesperus Press, please visit our website: **www.hesperuspress.com**